Beyond

A Course in Miracles

Sylvain du Boullay and Phoebe Lauren

ISBN 978-1461062752

There are those of us
who are being gently persuaded by Spirit
to move beyond A Course in Miracles.
The time has come for us
to move beyond the required course
to express the truth in a new way.
Now true knowledge is grasped.

This is beyond all words,
yet words are used still.

CONTENTS

PREFACE

The underlying basis of this book is *A Course in Miracles* (ACIM), a self-study metaphysical thought system that is unique in teaching forgiveness as the road to inner peace and the remembrance of the unconditional love of God. It consists of Text, Workbook for Students with a lesson a day, and the Manual for Teachers. The curriculum of the Course is both theoretical and practical with an emphasis on application rather than theory, and experience rather than theology. It specifically states that "a universal theology is impossible, but a universal experience is not only possible but necessary".

The authors have followed the teachings in ACIM as their spiritual path and were inspired to create this book, which you hold in your hands. It is offered to you as yet another possible aid to deepen your understanding of ACIM's basic concepts, as one more dispensable step along the journey without distance to the home that we never, in truth, have left.

Since this book, *Beyond A Course in Miracles*, was first published more than twenty years ago, there have been those who have questioned the meaning of the title. The word "beyond" was reluctantly added to the title when Phoebe had a vision in which the title was given to her. *"Beyond"* does not imply something superior or better than what the Course offers, as there can be nothing beyond what has already been written. Instead, the word "beyond" is used to emphasize that this book is another step along the path and that we must all eventually go "beyond" all that we know and all that we learn, for the final important step is taken in absolute willingness, trust, and faith. ACIM emphasizes that the Course "is a beginning, not an end."

CHAPTER ONE

THE COMING TOGETHER TO DO THIS WORK

Would we not recognize the deep call for love that we send to each other? Only love calls for love and love cannot fail to answer its own call. Take my hand and let's go home together.

THE COMING TOGETHER TO DO THIS WORK

This book, beyond words, was written by two people, a man and a woman, who did their very best to listen to inner guidance. They came from two very different places, both geographically and emotionally. They both had their own fantasies and illusions, which were played out through the relationship. In the end, they realized that one of the main reasons for their meeting and sharing was to write, even though this was not clear at first.

These two people are very much like you. They have had happy times and sad times. Each of them has managed to deal with his or her life – sometimes quite effectively and sometimes not. They are not special or different than you. The only reason they were able to give life to this book is that together they were able to keep the other's ego in check. The relationship, which was of great intensity for both of them, provided an opportunity for great learning and healing. In the initial stages of the joining, both experienced fear, frustration, and lack of trust. Imagine coming together with someone to do something and not knowing why. This is exactly what happened – yet they both remained willing to be open to God's plan.

1. The meeting together and waiting

Two people came together in a small town north of San Francisco to do God's work. Within the relationship, there were illusions to be sure – ones that played well upon the stage. Some were dense forms and, at times, disharmony and experiences of attack were presented. Eventually though, they both recognized the meaninglessness of the illusion. They began to see the illusions dissolve before their eyes as they watched each other play a perfect role.

After a relatively short time of sharing together, about three weeks, Phoebe received the first message which was written down through inner dictation from a voice. In part it said:

Mission: Share love throughout the world . . .
I cry out in this barren land – Jesus, Jesus, Jesus is his name. Dare you to step forward and utter such words? Are you ready to begin the journey without end – the journey without steps? It is that which is already completed in fact, but still apparently is a process to our minds.

We carry a torch of love and hope for all to see. We approach the world quietly and still. When we go now into the chaos, we do so silently like the fog drifting under the Golden Gate Bridge. No one will notice our coming. They will only feel our presence once we have arrived.

Now the movement begins. The life work has substance and meaning because we recognize it.

This was quite disturbing to Phoebe since it began with the name "Jesus". She shared with Sylvain that she did not believe the message and that she felt quite agitated. Sylvain, whose role was to try to be willing and trust, offered constant love and support to her. A few days later, on Christmas day, another message came. Phoebe asked the voice for guidance for them both and this was the answer received:

1. *We both know what we have to do together.*
2. *The plan is being revealed to us perfectly and in perfect time.*
3. *We can see only that which we no longer block.*
4. *The work is already complete. We are/were successful!*

And so the tension grew as they waited for more information. At times they were willing, at other times they were upset. But each time, it became clear that there was "something" to do together.

2. The agreement to write the book, which is already written in another dimension.

After many days of waiting, Phoebe began to have *strange* visions come to her in a meditative state as she recounts here:

"I was meditating and Jesus appeared to me. He was standing on the 7th of a series of steps. He was filled with love. I felt surprised and told him so. I could see that he was pouring forth constant love – so beautiful. He says he is the way home.

"I remember thinking that this must be a joke because I don't believe in Jesus. He again told me he loved me and that he was my way home. He explained that the distance to God was/is too great without him."

Some of you may feel offended by the title of this book and may even think that anyone who proposes such a title must certainly be arrogant. In fact, as mentioned in the Preface, the title was received by Phoebe under unusual circumstances, and she felt that she should be faithful to what was given. This happened a week later in a second meditation. Jesus again appeared and told her that a book would be written entitled: *Beyond A Course in Miracles.* She felt that a long time ago she had made a covenant with Jesus to do this work on earth and that now she was required to write.

The next day while she was meditating with Sylvain, Phoebe fell into a deep altered state. She found herself in a meadow playing with other children when Jesus came and called her. He said:

The book is already written. All you have to do is read it to make it come into this reality.

Phoebe was told that both she and Sylvain would *read and write* the book together. Phoebe received the chapter titles, and Sylvain began to organize the project. He suggested dating what was written and assured Phoebe that she could not fail. A few days later there was another appearance of Jesus. This time an internal dialogue took place as Phoebe continued to struggle with new ideas.

Jesus appeared on the 7th step of a stairway.

Jesus: I am the way home. Why do you continue to deny this?

Phoebe: Why do you continue to appear to me? I do not believe you are the way home. There are many ways to God and you are only one of them.
Jesus: I know why you say this. You have tried many ways. (Phoebe was then shown past lives where she was a monk, a Buddhist, and other religious lives.) *None of these ways brought you home. Why would you not want to go home a different way? I am the easiest way for you to reach God.*

Phoebe: That is a good question.

Other revelations came to Phoebe, making her increasingly agitated as she fought with what she was being guided to do. Sylvain saw clearly at this time as he wrote:

This book or whatever happens in the form is only a materialization of something. That something is real. This book is not.

You are real. Any form is not . . .

We have agreed to take this step together – to allow happiness to extend infinitely.

Both were clear that their coming together was not *personal*. It was a joining that transcended individuals. The direction they were given was always gentle and provided hope for them both.

Further clarification came from Jesus, which was entitled *Prelude*:

As long as you try to do something, you will not be able to do anything. What you are doing now directly with me is beyond all words and beyond all form. Though it all fits together and the sequence will become apparent – now in this present moment the only thing required of you is silence and willingness. To be willing means to be open in all ways to my word and its meaning.

You do not know that which you are called upon to do – there is a monumental task to which you are called. So be still now. Take some time to rejoice as the work begins. There is plenty of time to do everything. There is no reason to hurry or to try to do anything. Nothing can be missed - nothing can be left unsaid or undone if it is my will.

Rejoice in this happy recognition – that the time for peace on earth is present now. There has been a significant event on earth that has already occurred, though it is as yet unrecognized. Christ in truth has reappeared on earth. His presence is being felt everywhere, though as yet his presence goes without notice.

3. The struggle to believe in the work and its message

At this point, both began to shift from restlessness to a feeling of anticipation. Why were they chosen? What did all this mean? And most importantly, when would the actual work begin? The keynote word was *trust*. They constantly reminded each other to *know nothing* and not to ask worthless questions. This was a time of silence, a time of stillness. They both felt as if a whirlwind was about to strike. Sylvain wrote to calm Phoebe:

Trust your trust because nobody can trust for you, for there is nobody but you.

As the actual writing began, it became clear to them that it did not matter which one of them actually wrote the words on the page. Both of them had somehow already *read* them. It was common for Phoebe to comment that she was surprised Sylvain had put a certain section in one place when it really belonged somewhere else. Sometimes, she would be happy to *reread* a section and would be moved to tears. At other times, Sylvain would suddenly realize that he had left out something. During these times, they would both become quiet and wait while he *fixed* it by adding a word here and a sentence there. There were many mutual reassurances that nothing could be missed – nothing could be left unsaid or undone.

Sylvain wrote the following to Phoebe in the midst of the demands of taking down the book:

When you write, I immediately recognize my words. This is always exactly what I want to say. It makes total sense for me because in truth I have written it. Would you not hold my hand while I am writing?

You and I are two children. Our book is about love, nothing else. It is already written. It takes form in this dimension only through love and not through the finite mind, even though both our finite minds are used in a perfect blending combination.

Would we not recognize the deep call for love that we send to each other? Only love calls for love and love cannot fail to answer its own call. Take my hand and let's go home together.

And so they continued to work in love and towards their own deep healings. The wholeness of the plan became clearer as time went on.

4. *Just a little willingness*

Although Phoebe often questioned the contents of her voice's messages, she never questioned the identity or authenticity of the voice. She called it simply "my voice". Today, it has become "the voice". Many decisions were made by being still and listening to the voice. She was told that physical pain in her body manifested *every time you are not extending love – every time you try to be closed – you refuse to live what you know is true – every time you refuse to work on the book – every time you try not to remain on your specific pathway. Please stop hurting yourself, for no one else can hurt you. I am all love. Do not continue to separate yourself from me . . .*

So, the healing process deepened as they continued the work. Not only did they write this book, but they rewrote their own lives. They realized that peace was at hand – that suffering and fear could be left behind. They decided to trust and be willing to take each other's hand and to walk through the golden arches of truth.

Near the completion of the book, Sylvain wrote a letter to Phoebe, which in part is reproduced here:

. . .This book can only be written through love . . . The one condition for love to express itself openly in this world is willingness. The only question that each of us constantly asks the other is "Are

you willing?"

And I give thanks to you, beyond all that I know, for this question you never fail to ask me out of perfect love. We do know deep inside that the reading of this book is extremely simple. The slightest strain comes when we are not willing.

Are we, you Phoebe, and I Sylvain, going to strive for fear when peace is at hand?

Remember: We are constantly happy children laughing and playing in the meadows. Who is asking us to leave this place? Could it possibly be God? And who is there apart from God?

I only send you back the perfect love that you constantly send me.

And so the book was completed with infinite love and patience, and both were transformed by the experience. There was an awareness and a knowing that this shared endeavor involved much more than the writing of a book. It involved the joining of two people in Spirit, a coming together that was a pivotal point in each of their lives. This time spent together fulfilled a deep longing and a commitment. They were both destined to openly continue their spiritual work in the world, as they follow their individual spiritual paths.

CHAPTER TWO

THE UNDERSTANDING OF KNOWLEDGE
BEYOND WORDS

*Once we have chosen to go home, our goal is set
and aligned with the goal of Spirit and we cannot
fail to reach our destination. It is always our
choice to start the journey here and now.*

THE UNDERSTANDING OF KNOWLEDGE
BEYOND WORDS

The name Phoebe as such does not matter. As any name it is a symbol. In this world it is a symbol of light. Light is the condition of vision. Vision comes from the recognition of what is there. What is truly there is real and what is real is Love or God or Perfection.

You are real, so you are Love Itself. The recognition of what you are comes from experiencing it. Love is giving and receiving infinitely, thus making Itself empty and wholly full at the same "time". Being totally empty, It can receive everything. Being totally full, It can give everything.

When you think you know something, you do not think that you are totally empty. When you think you do not know something, you do not think that you are totally full. How can you, then, be aware of your being?

This awareness will come through healing. And this healing will take place through your relationship with your brother. For every brother you encounter, you are Phoebe, the light of the world, and so he is for you.

You have all the names. This means that your name is beyond sound, beyond form. Your name belongs to that place where there is no name, or rather where one name is all names because one is truly all. Yet, while in this World, be still and listen:

"Phoebe, you are the light of the world. It is only through me that you become aware of God, the Father. It is time to come home where all happiness abides. It is time right now to be happy. The clouds of darkness are lifted in this instant. It is now that Atonement begins – that "reality" becomes real.

"Do not attempt to understand this with your mind for it is not there that true knowledge lies. It is beyond this. True knowledge is not known with the finite mind. It is beyond all this. Knowledge comes when the ego no longer exists, when all trying and attempting to understand ceases because you cannot understand anything. You know nothing. The more you struggle to understand something – to make sense about some thing – the less you truly know.

"Knowledge comes from having a pure willingness to understand. A willingness to recognize once and for all that you cannot know anything by yourself. This is not possible. By having true willingness, all knowledge is immediately apparent. There is no thing that is unknowable – there is nothing that cannot be known by you. This comes through willingness.

"When you think you know something, you know nothing. No thought that you have ever had has been true. No thought that you will ever have is true. You cannot know the truth by your individual thought. This is not possible. Give up this idea, this thought once and for all. This is an ego trap, a useless notion that keeps you from knowing the truth. There is no way out by using your limited mind with its limited thoughts.

"Reality does not exist in your mind, in your thoughts, though you will make up many things. These things, which are made up, are illusions. They do not exist. They are the ego's way of keeping you from knowing the truth. Now the time has come for you to stop thinking these useless thoughts. They do not exist and they never existed. Still your mind and open your heart to the truth."

1. How do we truly understand something?

We have trained our mind to understand the meaning of what we see or think. We believe that through this training we do know something. We make up science and "wisdom", going from effect to effect, never finding a real cause to any effect. We constantly experience the feeling of having found something valuable, but soon we have to search further because that something, somewhere, somehow, has deceived us.

We do this because we decide to do it. To decide to do something means that we think that what we decide to do has value for us, whether we like to do it or not. A decision always comes from a belief. And to believe in something is thinking that this something is real. As long as we believe in the value of our finite mind and body, we think they are real. This means that limitations remain real to us. Thus do we make the world of limitations we see, and we cannot see beyond limitations; we cannot see what is real.

Reason will tell us that what is real has no limit. A limit is an end. What happens when something ends? At the very place where it ends, it is not there anymore and then, can we truly say that it does not exist. This is why we can never see the present with our finite mind, that mind which is not real but which we make real for us because we believe it is real. For us, the present is a constant symbol of ending or death. How can we see what is real and never ends, when all our striving aims at searching for the meaning of something that constantly dies?

As "human" beings we have limited vision. What does "human" mean? It means belonging to a body, identifying with a body. A body is meant to be somewhere in time and space. A body sees, hears, tastes, touches and smells things that are not itself. By definition it is separate. The finite mind is part of the body, and we believe that we really think with our finite mind. Now, what can the finite mind see or think? Only finite things, things which end, things which die; only finite thoughts, thoughts which end, thoughts which die. These things and thoughts do not really exist. Yet they exist *for* us, they exist in our illusion of the reality of our finite belief system. How could we truly understand anything real with such a belief system?

To understand is to find a meaning and a meaning relates to a cause. The concept of a cause implies a natural and true relation between cause and effect. An effect does not create its cause. A cause creates effect automatically because of the very nature of the cause. An effect *has to be* when its cause exists.

Given these premises about cause and effect, let us approach now this "something" that we are trying to understand. We are trying to understand the cause of everything. As we believe everything dies, we strive to understand the cause of death. Now, what could be the cause of death if not death itself? What could create death automatically because of its very nature if not absence itself, or non-beingness or nothingness?

Yet, the only thing of what we are sure of now is that we can truly say: "I live", meaning "I am", meaning also "I am not dead". We look for its cause among limited and illusory effects with our limited and illusory finite mind, both of which are not real because they both end somewhere. Believing in death, we believe we are separated from life. Making death real, we look for its cause, which by definition is not there. Either life or death is true, but not both for they are incompatible. This is why the only question the ego is constantly asking is "How did the impossible occur?" not seeing the fundamental contradiction in this question to which there is no answer because the question itself is meaningless. This question really means: "How can the dead be alive?"

The only *real* question is "What is the cause of life?" Whoever asks this question has to be alive. So this question really means, "Who am I?" And to find an answer to this question, we must go beyond our finite mind and be aware of what is real *now*. We must let Reality – or Life – or God – or I – reveal Itself to us through our present experience. We must go beyond understanding to true awareness.

2. How can we go beyond understanding to true awareness?

Understanding implies cause and effect. It is a process that consists of going from an effect to its cause. It implies "somebody" who thinks and through this thinking recognizes the cause of the effect. It implies that this "somebody" is separated from the effect and its cause.

Being aware is a state and not a process. It does not imply movement. It does not imply a cause and an effect. It is whole and self sustained.

True awareness means awareness of what is real and what is real is love and only love. The ego itself is a state of awareness, but it is an awareness of what is not real, what is not true, what contradicts itself. There are only two states: the ego and full awareness. And there are only two emotions: love and fear. When we speak about love here, we do not refer to the limited "love" of the world that is anything but love. We refer to the total giving and total receiving. We refer to infinity or oneness.

So it is that to be aware of love, we have to be love itself. We have to be aware of infinity. And to be aware of the ego, we have to be the ego itself with all that it implies: fear, guilt, pain and death. We have to be aware of a finite state. We cannot be aware of both a finite state and infinity. One excludes the other. In this world, we think we are the ego – or a finite state. Understanding is part of this finite state and we need to go beyond understanding to be fully conscious of our infinite state. This full consciousness is true awareness. How then, can we go beyond the finite state of understanding to true awareness?

We have to do this in the state in which we are, which is a finite state of movement. This is why we speak of "going back" home to that place we never left. We have to start on a journey without distance which does not really exist but in which we believe. What is this journey?

This journey is undertaken in time and space. It starts somewhere, sometime, lasts for a while, and ends somewhere at some time. Where and when does this journey start, last and end?

It starts only when we are willing to start it. Without our willingness, there is no journey back home. This is why willingness has the first place in time in God's plan. To be willing is the only choice we have to make. It is our sole function.

We can elect what journey we want to take at any given time, but we cannot choose the route. There are only two journeys. Both present millions of different aspects in time and space and might appear totally different for each one of us. Both have one goal. One is of the world and leads to death. The other is not of the world and leads us home. To choose one of them is our choice and there is no other choice. We are choosing one of them every moment. This choice starts our journey.

Once we have chosen to go home, our goal is set and aligned with the goal of Spirit and we cannot fail to reach our destination. It is always our choice to start the journey here and now. Once the choice is made, we never know how long and where the journey will take us. We never know where and when it will end. If we knew this, there would be no need for this journey. We only know that our goal is true happiness. And we accept the reaching of this goal as soon as we have the slightest willingness to have our will for happiness aligned with God's Will. Willingness is the first step towards true awareness and is truly the only step there is. Along the journey we will find ourselves more and more willing until we are wholly willing for the last step taken by God. This last step is a sudden shift to knowledge, which is often referred to as enlightenment.

3. What is knowledge?

Knowledge is of God. Knowledge is a state of perfect peace, perfect happiness, perfect love and perfect joy. Knowledge is referred to as the "vision of God". Yet it cannot be the kind of vision we know of. This is because in our state we believe perceptions are real. Perception implies a perceiver and a perceived. It implies two separate beings. God, being all there is, can *not* perceive Himself. God can only experience God. This experience is the only experience there is. It is totally spiritual, which means that it does not depend on any form. It is totally beyond time and space.

We are created by God. Creation is extension. This means that God does not leave His Creation. He totally gives Himself to His Creation. Creation is perfect movement in perfect stillness. Perfect Movement proceeds from Perfect Stillness. Perfect Movement is the Son of Perfect Stillness. Perfect Movement is Perfect Stillness.

Being God's creation, we are like our Creator, perfect and infinite. Like our Creator, we create and our creations are perfect and infinite. We cannot grasp this with our finite mind because our finite mind knows only of God *and* us, or us *and* our brother. Even when we say that God created us, it does not really make sense to us because we still believe we are separated from God. Yet, this idea of being the perfect creation of the perfect Creator is essential for us to attain knowledge.

We attain knowledge by going closer to knowledge step by step. In truth we do not have to attain knowledge because we are that very state of perfection. Yet, in this world of illusion, we have made the ego state – or separation – real for us, and we have forgotten our state. We then need this illusory journey that leads us closer and closer to knowledge. This journey brings us a gradual awareness of love's eternal presence.

To love truly is to be willing to receive and give *everything*. Let us still our mind an instant and realize what happens when we love truly. We can then truly say: "I *give* everything, all there is, all my thoughts, all that I value. I keep nothing." And we add: "I am totally open, I deny nothing, I judge nothing, I accept everything, I *receive* everything." Then do we begin to realize that giving and receiving are the same. But we have realized this only because we have gone beyond limits. If we go back to a thought of limitation, which we constantly do, we immediately fear that this total giving and receiving will hurt us. We feel that if we give way, all that is not us will immediately rush and take advantage of us. Thus have we "lost" the way because we have not been totally willing.

Yet we can still say "I am willing now". We can always be willing now, for it is always now. As soon as we choose again to be willing, we are immediately back on the way home, going closer and closer to knowledge.

The last step, which is the state of knowledge itself, is taken by God. God is beyond time. So, in truth, God has already taken this last step for us. We are not aware of this as long as we are not wholly willing to let go of our beliefs. Our constant willingness allows Spirit to undo *in time* our beliefs in limitation, step by step, all along our journey home. This journey ends in a sudden and joyous realization that there was no journey. Then we are back to perfect peace in timelessness.

4. How do we know that we are in a state of knowingness rather than an ego state?

The ego state is not real. It is a belief in something that does not exist. In fact we are permanently in a state of knowingness. This is why we are called to see only perfection in any brother. We are not called to this by some punishing god or by some external threatening law. We are called to see it by perfection itself which is always calling for love because love calls only for itself.

However, as long as we believe in the ego, we constantly see signposts of both the ego state and the state of knowingness. These signposts carry messages that bear witness to one of the two states. These signposts are held out by messengers we have sent. These messengers are our thoughts. What is a thought?

A thought is never in the past, nor in the future. A thought is now, thus being beyond time. A thought is either a creation of the Universal mind or a "making" – or projection – of the finite mind. The "part" of the mind that creates is the real mind. In fact only this "part" exists. But the "unthinkable" thought of separation produces the illusion of another part of the mind that makes up finite things or illusions. Illusions are "real" to this unreal part of the mind. This is how we believe, as a finite body, to be our own author, thus loosing sight of our eternal beingness.

To think is to see now. We can only see now with one of the two emotions, love or fear. Not both. We all know deep inside of us what thinking without fear is. This is because we are one with the perfect Thought. Yet, the "unthinkable" thought of separation has veiled this oneness. This mad thought, instead of creating, makes up illusions like itself. This is why we identify with a body. When we do this, we receive messages of fear and guilt. We feel unhappy.

The only way for right thinking to come is from stillness, from letting go in that one instant that we call the present. Actually we constantly do this, but because of our belief in separation – in finite things – we soon go back to fear and anxiety. To escape this process, we have to be aware of it. Then can we be consciously willing to let it go.

So it is that there are only two kinds of thoughts. Some are real and some are not. The ones which are not real do not matter as such, but they matter *for us* and we must not turn away from them, thus hiding them and keeping them from disappearing. As surely as a real thought is creation, an unreal thought is a mistake which needs correction at its level but does not really exist. If we are not willing to bring this mistake to the light to let the One Mind correct it, it will not be corrected because we *are* the One Mind and nothing can be done to us without our will. This is what is meant by "every kingdom divided against itself is brought to desolation".

As long as we identify however slightly with our body, we cannot be aware of our creations. Creations are infinite in number and yet remain one in truth. Creations are real. Creations are the eternal extension of God – or Reality – in timelessness. Creations are limitless movement in perfect stillness. The awareness of being a creation implies the awareness of being ever creating, the awareness of God ever creating. This is alien to body identification. What is the meaning of this tiny little speck of dust called a body versus the awareness of the One Creator and creations as one? This is why the journey home ends in a magnificent and happy laughter, a pure crystal laughter that nothing can disturb.

In this world, the signposts that we constantly see are our internal feelings. We always experience *now* one of two emotions: love or fear. This gives us a sense of happiness or unhappiness. We think that this happiness or unhappiness comes from external circumstances. These circumstances are any event that seems to happen now or that happened in the past or will happen in the future. If we judge these events "good" we feel some kind of happiness, if we judge them "bad" we feel unhappiness. We have to be aware that we keep judging everything we see.

When we judge something as good versus bad, or

as bad versus good, we literally separate from what is judged. And this separation implies that we do not control what is judged. When we think that we have total control over "something", we consider this "something" as entirely neutral and we cannot be affected by it.

Let us examine closer where this leads us. We feel happy or unhappy according to how we judge external circumstances, and we feel that we have no control over circumstances. This brings a great deal of fear. So do we fight and battle to gain control. Thus do we make hell because our striving ultimately fails and we fear more and more. The very fact of seeing this process is the proof of the ego's failure. This, the ego does not want you to see at any cost. This cost includes the insane belief in the value of sacrifice. You have to sacrifice yourself or others to prove that something "better" exists.

The ultimate "loving" sacrifice is to die for a god, thus "proving" that the ego was right, thus making the ego itself a god. To make a god means to build up the idea of a mighty being, so mighty that all other beings are nothing but miserable and valueless sinners. The greater the separation between this god and all other beings, the more the ego has the illusion to please this monster it has made, so that the monster will not kill it but rather save it for its "loving" sacrifice. On one hand, the ego makes every effort to make up an idol or a god as mighty as possible to prove itself to be a mighty "creator". On the other hand, it fears more and more that this god will kill it for its "sins". This is insanity.

We see now that if we keep looking outside for external circumstances to "save" us, we end up in hell. Yet, if we watch carefully and honestly our internal feelings, we become aware of a state of happiness which is not related to external circumstances. The more we go inside, which means to be still and to listen, the more we are aware of "something" unknown and wholly loving which never leaves us. It is by internally experiencing the unknown that we become aware of being in a state of knowingness. We then begin to see that we are more and more willing and more and more trusting. We are more aware that our happiness does not come from our finite mind and has nothing to do with forms such as words and our striving to build up theories out of them. We begin to know that we are beyond words and theories. We begin to feel internally our need to let go of the known, to be still and listen to that part in us which is totally unknown but never leaves us.

5. Why do we need to use words when we are really beyond them?

A word is a sound, a written form or a sign, which happens here and now and which brings remembrance of something through our memory. We can say, write or make signs, thus sending – or offering – words. We can hear or read them, thus "receiving" them. In this world, words are used to communicate. Communication is only possible where there is a sender *and* a receiver. If one of them does not want to give or to receive, communication is impossible.

In Heaven – or the awareness of being one with God – there is pure or direct communication. There are no symbols and no words because there is no memory. There is an infinite and immediate communication that is infinitely giving and receiving at the same "time". We are now truly in Heaven and we do communicate directly without words in timelessness.

To communicate is to share a thought. In Heaven we constantly share the One Thought with no second, no third. It is pure love, ever creating. We are the Thoughts of the One Thought. We are the Son of God. We are God Himself extending Himself.

In this world, we share thoughts by words. These thoughts are not real because they refer to our memory. Yet, when we let Spirit guide us, these thoughts are used to show us how insane is the world of separation that we have made.

Words lead us to the past, to the known. However, because we have a deep sense of what we are, which is pure love, communication by words is used by Spirit to remind us of our natural state. This is how we become gradually aware of communicating without words, thus sharing true love.

The words used have to be perfectly clear, otherwise they mislead us, they bring us back to confusion. We have to know what we are saying and we have to know the meaning of what we hear. Clarity is essential.

Clarity is the absence of contradiction. Contradiction is conflict. Contradiction is meaningless. Clarity is meaningful. When we indulge in contradiction, we accept as true two things that exclude one another. On our way home, we need clear words to help us stay on the right path. Yet this path leads us beyond words. This path ends with the One Word, which is the last step which is taken by God Himself. Until this last step, we are guided by words, clear words, spoken with reason, showing us the way. Yet on the way itself there is only an experience of love, which becomes more and more frequent. Both hearing the words and experiencing their meaning is necessary.

The ego is very consistent in its own thought system. But its thought system is based on lies, on admitting the reality of things that exclude one another. Clear words are used to show us the unreality of what we think we are and of what we think of as good or bad. Words invite us to question the sanity of the ego. And this we have to do if we want to escape this fearful world. This is why a course in miracles is required. A course in miracles leads us to the unlearning of what we have taught ourselves. This unlearning takes different avenues for each one of us. There is a different course in miracles for each of us. This is why a book about this unlearning could not be called *"The" Course in Miracles*, but *"A" Course in Miracles*.

Yet, the core of any course in miracles is always the same: God's Son is guiltless and in his innocence lies his salvation. This means: You and I are this one Son of God, created perfect and safe, perfectly loved and perfectly loving eternally. *A Course in Miracles* is then a tool made of words inviting us, through reason and experience combined, to face the error we made and to accept the gift of God. This is done in time by using the present avenues. By using them in the right way we come closer and closer to God or rather we become more and more aware of God and our Sonship. The present world gradually loses its attraction and we become more aware of the real world, which is totally loving. We begin to recognize God's gift to us.

6. God's gift to us: What is it and how do we recognize it?

What can God give except Himself? God's gift is God Himself and God has already given *all* of Himself. Still we feel that we have to accept something that is offered to us. Why? This is because of our belief in lack. We believe we are limited, weak and sinful. To sin means to do something we should not do. It means failure. This failure brings guilt, fear and pain. And because we make what we believe in, we make sickness and death. The only way out of this is to accept the knowledge of who we are. We have to accept true knowledge.

What is true knowledge? It is to know that *we are one with God*. If we stay in the ego's thought system, this statement appears to be highly fearful because we made up a god which is everything we are not. This god is all mighty and we are insignificant sinners. Saying, then, that we are one with this "god" appears to be highly arrogant and does not make sense.

God really gives us nothing. Being all there is, what is it that is not of Him? And being total Love, what is it that He has not given? What has He kept for Himself? He is infinite. He is perfect love, ever loving what He creates like Himself – infinite and perfect. This our finite mind cannot grasp. Yet reason will tell us that it cannot be otherwise.

There cannot be infinity *and* something apart. Love cannot keep anything apart from Itself. Love can only extend Itself forever, thus receiving forever. This is why God waits for our return *only* in our mind, only in time and space, but not in reality. *We are one with God.*

What we call God's gift is all there is. And all there is, is rightfully ours. Having and being are the same for, in truth, we are what we have and we have what we are. To be rightfully ours means that everything is ours because of the nature of what really exists. Its nature being total love, it is totally given to everyone. Now what is it that is given?

What is given is real, so it is eternal. Can a form be eternal? No, because a form happens in time and space. Only Spirit is real. So what is given is infinite creative thought. This infinite creative thought is infinite peace and bliss. And this is what is rightfully ours because this is what we constantly receive and constantly give.

Now do we see that we can only recognize God's gift by knowing who we are. And knowing who we are is knowledge. Yet understanding knowledge is not knowledge. Knowledge is beyond words. Understanding happens in time and space. Understanding comes from the rightful use of words. Knowledge comes when the use of words combined with our willingness to experience them has ultimately brought us home. This is the sudden shift from perception to knowledge. This shift is of God, not of man.

*7. How can this understanding of knowledge help
me in my decision making process?*

Here I am, having to decide what to say and what
to do. For this I have to understand what is the
intention of God. An intention is a decision or will.
Knowing that I am perfect like God, I must admit
that my will cannot be apart from God's, even if
external circumstances seem to keep telling me
that my intentions are not at all like His. I must
realize that all my desires conflict, but God's do
not. I must realize that I really know nothing and
then wait for knowledge to come by itself. How is
this done?

The intention of God has to be perfectly clear to
me. As long as I think that God wants something
from me, I believe in sin. This is because I believe
perfection wants something perfect from
something that is not perfect. It is impossible. If I
believe this, I admit that I am a sinner, incapable
of doing what I am asked to do.

When I clearly see that God's will for me is that I
know who I am, and when I also see that I cannot
know anything by myself, I choose to listen and
wait for knowledge. I choose to listen to the Voice
for God, which never fails to speak to me. What is
the Voice for God?

God being Spirit, His Voice can only be Spirit and
can only be heard by the mind. As long as I believe

a body or a form is telling me something by itself, I keep looking outside of myself for an answer. I have to realize that whatever I hear I only hear what I want to hear. If I choose to hear separation, fear, guilt, pain and death, I hear it. If I choose to hear the unknown part of my mind, which constantly speaks to me out of total love, I hear it.

What happens when I choose to hear this unknown part of my mind? Choosing to hear the unknown is to be totally open. It is a total letting go of the past and my illusions of safety through attack. To attack is to want to change something, to kill or suppress something I do not want. As I do not want to be as I perceive myself, I constantly want to kill myself. Yet, at the same time I want to love and be happy. This brings tremendous conflict. The only way out of this is to stop wanting to be alone, separate. Then, and only then, am I open to real communication.

When I am truly open, it gradually becomes my experience that I take correct action without striving. I begin to experience what is a true relationship and more and more things and events begin to make sense to me. To be truly open is to be available for anything. For the thinking of the world it is the most dangerous thing. Yet, I begin to sense that it is the safest thing that can happen to me.

This new understanding of knowledge, which

grows in me, begins to bring a new sense of peace and happiness. I begin to see miracles happen by themselves. I begin to sense harmony everywhere. I really begin to know that everything, every event and circumstance is for my own best interest. Then I know that I always take correct action. I also know that any brother I meet or think of also takes correct action according to his present state of mind. I see myself less and less judgmental. I constantly experience the tremendous healing power of love. This becomes for me a pearl of great price that nobody can take away from me. This pearl of great price is not a form. It is the Cause of the effects I perceive rightfully. I begin to realize that all that I see brings me peace and happiness because of my inner attitude of complete *trust*. I have discovered that trusting myself or rather my Self is the only loving attitude there is.

CHAPTER THREE

HOW CAN WE TRUST IN THIS WORLD OF CHAOS?

It is only by being willing now that we let our goals be aligned to the goals of Spirit. Thus do we allow miracles to happen, transcending time and space. Every single miracle has already been given. It only waits upon our willingness to manifest itself in time and space.

HOW CAN WE TRUST IN THIS WORLD OF CHAOS?

To be willing is a gift. God tells us to trust Him and we will be saved. What is it "to be saved" – what does God mean by this? To be saved means to come home again, to go back to that which we never left. How is it that in this world of chaos, we can be led to speak of such things? This is a question that many people have asked me. As long as I believe that this world exists, that it has a reality of its own, I am sure that I exist in a world of complete chaos. It is a world gone mad – a world that is beyond comprehension. However, this world that I see and that I believe in is not real. That which is not real cannot and does not exist.

Well then, what is the way out of this situation? How can we stop seeing the world as a chaotic place? How can we in this moment go home to the "real" world where nothing can be threatened?

1. What does it mean to trust?

For the world, to trust is always to trust somebody – or rather some body – or some thing. I would trust a person because this "person" has never or rarely deceived me, or I would trust some thing because this thing has never failed. Thus I always refer to the past and I hope the future will be the same. I have taught myself to do this because it is through my past experiences that I seem to feel a sense of security. I constantly sort out elements of my past to judge them fairly reliable and I project them into the future to make them happen again. The whole safety of the world is based on this process.

This process leads to the making up of idols. As long as I identify myself as belonging to this world of chaos, I go from idol to idol in a desperate attempt to find some security. As this world is made up of finite things and finite bodies, I constantly change my idols. I constantly look outside to check that a certain number of people have the same idols as mine. This is how groups, parties and gatherings are generally set up.

Now real trust is totally alien to the thinking of the world. For the ego, real trust is the most frightening thing because it relies on nobody – no body – and nothing – no thing. It is the symbol of total insecurity. Still, no one is totally alien to real trust. There is no one who does not deeply long for it. If we honestly consider this, we find there a witness to our real nature, to the gift that God has given us, and which nothing or nobody can take away from us. Somewhere, somehow we *know* what trust is, and we long to trust, feeling inwardly that it is the only way to peace.

To trust means to be willing. And it takes great learning – or rather unlearning – to really be willing, to really understand that true security comes from what the world calls total insecurity. Yet there is no one who does not know this. It is the belief in the value finite things can bring that has temporarily obscured it. And it is only by gradually letting go of this belief that real trust can replace trust in what the physical eyes see.

It must be understood that trust has nothing to do with courage which is a state related to the thinking of the world. Courage implies fear. To have courage is to accept fear as inevitable. It implies the belief in danger, harm, pain and death. To really trust is beyond courage. To understand this we must realize "what" it is we trust.

If we do not trust some body or some thing, and if we do know that we trust "something", what is this something? To understand this, we must realize that *we* have to trust for ourselves and that no one else can trust for us. Thus, do we understand that we trust in our Self, in that part inside us that says "I". It is thus that we trust in God. But this time it is not a god that we make up with finite concepts, but the One God or perfection. We trust Reality. We trust infinite Beingness. We totally trust the present and we are no longer concerned with past or future. This state, which is our natural state, is totally alien to the thinking of the world. Understanding this is the only way out of this world. And we cannot fail to find this way out for we are it. This is why he who has found it can truly say, "I am the way".

2. Why does the world of chaos not really exist?

For the ego or the sense of separation, nothing is more real than this world. What we call the ego is a belief, a whole thought system that appears very complicated and very well organized. Its survival depends entirely on its complexity, its defenses and attacks. Yet, its foundation or cornerstone is very simple. It is the belief that every single thing or person or thought is private and has an existence of its own which can be improved or damaged.

Now, what can improve or damage it? It is the ego itself, which is the very identification to a private body and a private mind, separate from other bodies and minds, separate from every single thing that appears in this continual illusion. This belief has to make time real, because of its goal which is to protect itself from weakness, pain and death. It has to work out continuously some plan to replace a former plan that does not work. The ego, then, has to go from illusion to illusion in a vain attempt to find security by projecting itself into the future, thus trying to make it "better" than the past or at least the same.

This continual illusion makes up the "dream" in time. And this dream has a great strength of its own. Unless the whole process of continuously striving to hide the truth is seen, no one can get out of this dream, which is extremely well organized in its madness. One has to see why it is so well organized.

The "work" the ego is doing seems "noble", "good", "efficient" and "reasonable" because the ego admits that this world somewhere, somehow, is chaotic. Then, what more "noble" task is there than striving with all of one's strength and "heart" to get rid of this chaos? The ego's sole error is to believe that it can do something about it with its own "strength". The "strength" of the ego is total weakness and helplessness because its entire being is based on separation. By separating itself, by constantly making up differences, it makes itself weaker and weaker and in fact goes surely to death. The more it strives to find a way out, the more it receives messages from this chaotic existence.

So it is that its only "way out" of this is through pain, suffering and struggle that become "necessary". Suffering brings a "reason" to fight, an illusion that this fighting will bring something valuable that will make the future better than the past. Then it seems "noble" and necessary to attack everything and everyone for having been guilty (to attack). And everyone seen as limited is seen by essence as forced to attack. The ego then sorts out, through private judgment, groups and categories of people, friends, or relatives who have been attacked and "need" protection. A tremendous amount of guilt is projected upon what has attacked them and the ego seems to "prove" its innocence and value by literally killing the "sinners".

The strength of this whole process has to be seen for what it is: total weakness, insignificance – or rather: nothing. This is merely because the whole process tends toward destroying and killing, though it wishes to build up and construct. The very fact of seeing this process wipes out the guilt and what is seen then is just a temporary mistake. It has to be a mistake because in spite of this constant destruction "something" does exist and this "something" has nothing to do with the world of destruction. Moreover, you cannot have both this "something" and the world of chaos. One has to be true and the other false or not real. Reason will tell you which is which. The very fact of seeing the dream as a dream shows then that we are in the dream but not of it.

3. What is it that God really wants us to see and experience?

What God really wants us to see and experience is what He is. As God is perfection and all there is, we cannot truly see and experience anything else. What *is* cannot be attacked or destroyed. It is wholly safe and self sustained. Now, why is it that this can only be bliss or ecstasy?

Pain and suffering arise from experiencing something that we do not want, something that we would like to be different. Now, if we truly experience a state in which nothing has to be changed and nothing is desired, this state has to be perfect happiness. This is because "imperfect" happiness would be a happiness which could be improved, a state in which something would have to be changed or adjusted to reach perfection. It would imply the very idea of a need somewhere and this state would not be God. It would be totally alien to God, for you cannot have both perfection and imperfection. Each one totally excludes the other. So it is that either God exists and there can be only perfection, or God does not exist and there can be only chaos. Yet we have seen that chaos cannot exist because it embodies the very idea of destruction, and nothing then would exist. Now do we begin to realize that what exists can only be whole and total and bring nothing with it but an experience of bliss and ecstasy. This is the realm of creation or Heaven. This is Love.

Yet, how do we know what God wants? The answer to this question is very simple: we do know what God wants when we know what *we* truly want. And we know what we truly want when we realize that as long as we believe in the reality of the world of chaos we do not truly know what we want. We only seem to know it because we strive with all our strength to escape the fact that all our desires conflict. The ego does not want to see this because it would be the end of its "existence", the end of *its* way of finding security and happiness. The ego constantly strives for happiness. However, because of the illusion which it is made of, it is very clever to hide at all cost the very fact that it comes from an illusion and that its ways can only lead to despair and death. This it does not want to see because it does not believe in perfection here and now. When we still believe in the value imperfection can bring, we fear to let go of chaos *because we fear to lose the defenses we believe in.*

Yet, as we all remain aware somewhere deep inside us of our infinite nature, we cannot fail to gradually move to joy. It is through our experiences that we become more and more aware that there must be another way out of this. And this is not through our striving with our intellect, even though the intellect is used for this. In Heaven there is no intellect but only infinite knowledge. Yet, in this world the intellect is used when it is offered to Spirit or to the One Teacher for Him to use in His way.

As soon as we become willing, we begin to experience a more happy existence or rather a more happy dream. We become more and more aware of God's plan unfolding. We feel happier and more secure. Events and encounters make more sense. The journey towards the moment of recognition has begun. For this journey time is used, which means that the dream itself is used as a way out of the dream. The illusions themselves are used in time to allow us to recognize them as illusions. Thus are the blocks to the awareness of love's presence gradually removed until the moment of recognition happens by itself in time, until vision suddenly dawns on us and time disappears, being no longer useful. Then we are back home and we know that we can never be away from it because we *are* it.

4. How can I go home to that place which I never left?

If the truth is that I never left home, then I must be home now. Why is it then that I am not aware of being home? This is because I constantly project myself in the past or in the future. I "make up" myself by looking into the past and judging it, and I choose among my past experiences those that I want to avoid, alter or reproduce. These experiences have never brought me real peace and happiness. Yet I still believe that there are "good" and "bad" ones.

So it is that the only way to know that I am home now is to stop this constant process between past and future. In other words, I must be fully present. To be fully present means to not judge the present, to not compare it with a past, which is gone, and a future, which is not here yet. The only way to do this is to listen to God's Voice – or my higher self – which constantly tells me what is real and wholly peaceful now.

When I project myself in the past or in the future, I project myself into a place that is not real by definition because it is not there. This is the reason why the past in truth never happened. What we think has happened is only a dream that we make now, an illusion in which we believe.

When we stop all judgment, we are able to see

creation's messages moment to moment. To understand this, let us watch carefully what happens when we do this. We all have had these experiences of real peace. They might not have lasted long but let us see what they show us now. An experience of real peace gives us a sense of harmony. Now, where is judgment when we experience harmony? What do we want to change, to improve or to alter? What do we want to attack? Are we then thinking of the past or of the future? In others words, are we desiring anything? All these preoccupations have gone and we truly see with our mind the messages of creation. These messages are joy, peace, love, quietness and happiness. We do not have to strive with our intellect to be aware of them.

Now why do they seem to disappear so quickly? This is because of our belief system. We have trained ourselves to judge everything and to try to protect and keep every "good" situation with our own limited strength. Then, we immediately "go" to the future and start making up a plan to reproduce this sense of harmony. We do not realize that in doing this, we bring in fear. We believe in failure and we fear that if we do not strive, this situation might not happen again. And in fact we make up at the same time both a similar situation *and* its opposite, which is a painful situation. This is according to the law that we make real for us what we believe in. As long as we believe in good *and* evil, we will experience good *and* evil.

So it is that the only way to find harmony and peace is to join in holy relationships. A holy relationship is holy because it is true. And being true it is real. Because it is real it is fully in the present and it does not know of any fear. A holy relationship in which I join implies that I do not expect anything from the other and do not feel guilty about anything from my interaction with him or her in the past. This is done through forgiveness. Forgiveness is to not give reality to what seems to have happened, and to truly see that the other is ever sinless. This means that any sense of judgment about another is entirely a mistake that we make. A mistake merely needs correction. And this correction we cannot make because we still believe somehow in the value of finite things. This is the reason why we have to constantly offer our relationship to Him Who knows of infinity. This we do through trusting. Yet we might feel that we do not know how to trust and there we see again that it is only through our willingness that we will let Him show us that complete and total trust has never left us because of our Source.

We do not have to wait to be willing. If we say "I shall be willing when I go through a therapy, when I get out of this dreadful financial situation or when I meet the companion I have been searching for so long", we merely refuse the gift of God which He cannot force us to accept. It is only by being willing *now* that we let our goals be aligned to the goals of Spirit. Thus do we allow miracles to happen, transcending time and space. Every single miracle has already been given. It only waits upon our willingness to manifest itself in time and space. Miracles are milestones on our way home. They open us to the fact that we do transcend time and space.

5. What are the three basic elements to trust?

The first element to trust is *willingness*. When you really trust, you trust in no particular thing or person. You are willing to learn of the unknown. You open yourself to whatever might come. This is done through prayer and meditation. Prayer is not something you do to get something. It is a state in which you ask to see what is there and not what your physical eyes show you. Prayer comes as soon as you are willing. True prayer is saying: "Father, I want to see, and You are going to show me what is there because this is Your will". Then comes meditation which is pure listening. Meditation is not using a particular form for a particular result. The world knows of a kind of meditation that is not pure. It is listening in order to acquire something for your own private "good". By this process you remain stuck in your illusions because you strive to hear what you think you want and not what God wants. True meditation is necessary because it is the only way to hear God's answer to your prayer. This requires total stillness.

The second element to trust is *forgiveness*. Forgiveness is merely not judging. When you judge, you do not trust. You merely give a positive or negative value to whatever you judge. For many of us forgiveness is a word that takes great learning to understand. Until it is fully understood, we think that evil is somewhere, somehow, necessary and that we have to admit its reality and fight it with courage. Then we would say: "You, God, or you, my brother, you have done this thing to me, but I forgive you because I am "better" than you. I "love" you so much that I accept to suffer for you so that you can be happy." This belief has a great power of its own which we must not underestimate.

Usually the total understanding of forgiveness takes the three following steps:

First, we forgive our brothers. We come to the point where we recognize that our brothers have really done nothing wrong to us and that our frustration comes from our own belief.

Then we go on to the second step which is to really forgive ourselves for our misperceptions. This is what is meant by loving ourselves in a selfless way. In most cases this seems to be a much more difficult step. It might seem for a long time that guilt, which has been withdrawn from our brothers, has been laid upon us. We feel intense guilt for misperceiving.

Then comes the third step, which is very carefully hidden by the ego. This third step is forgiving God for what God has not done to us. We easily admit the idea that God is perfection but we do not admit the idea that we *are* perfection because of our Source. This is again a question of identity or authorship. We believe we have to make ourselves better in order to please a punishing god. We believe that we *have* to become perfect with some striving of our own. This is why we have to forgive God for what God has not done to us. Forgiving God is merely recognizing that perfection can only create perfection and that our brothers and ourselves are perfect because it is the Will of God, for we can only be in the likeness of our Source.

These three steps in the understanding of forgiveness might seem to follow each other in time but they are taken simultaneously, for if one of them is fully taken, the two others are fully taken too.

The third element to trust is *love*. Love seems to come from willingness and forgiveness, but we can also say that willingness and forgiveness come from love. In the process of removing the blocks to the awareness of love's presence, it seems that willingness and forgiveness have to come first. This is merely because it is a process of undoing. In fact this process is possible *because* of the presence of love which is First, with no second, no third. In the full awareness of the presence of love, there is no willingness, nor forgiveness. Both have served a purpose for learning in time and space and they disappear when time and space cease to be necessary for learning.

Yet, in the learning process, love seems to be an element of trust because, for a certain time, love seems to be not quite perfect. Love is inner peace and it is only gradually that we become aware of this inner peace. To attain it we begin to see that we *must* love ourselves in a selfless way. We also *must* join and believe in others. We *must* choose another way, which is the same as saying that we must choose to be ourselves.

Now, why is it that we cannot see alone who we are? Why is it that we need to do this through relationships? When we do not know who we are, it has to be because we think we are separate. Then our being does not make sense and is experienced as painful. It is only by experiencing what a holy or real relationship is that we can know we are not separate. We have to experience it and this experience becomes the one universal experience. This is why every brother we meet is truly our savior. He really brings with him a new opportunity to see that he is nothing but total love and total perfection. It is only with the experience of holy relationships that we can know we are one with each other and with God.

6. What can I do practically in my everyday life to become more trusting?

Now we see ourselves having to live an everyday life. We see a chaotic world but we are willing to trust more. How can we do this? We can only do this with what we have. And what we have, we have it now and not in the past or in the future. This is why the only way to become more trusting is to be more attentive or vigilant to the present.

When we do this, we start experiencing new signs. These signs have always been there, but because we are more still, we gradually become more aware of them. Now, what are these signs? They are miracles. A miracle is an effect and it is by seeing this effect that we become aware of its Source. Miracles happen in time. This is why, as such, they do not matter, for what happens in time is not eternal and therefore not real. Yet we can say that they are the only reality in the dream, or rather they are the only part of the dream that leads to the undoing of the dream. We realize this when we truly see that there is no order of difficulty in miracles. The first principle of any course in miracles is fundamental, even though it might seem the hardest to grasp. No order of difficulty in miracles really means that the world is truly saved. And if we think that we and the world are not saved, it has to do with our perceptions. This is why we have to be willing to have our perceptions changed.

So, on one side we know intellectually that there is no order of difficulty in miracles, but on the other side, we do not really believe it. So it is that we are led to proceed step by step with the process of undoing. At first we are led to trust this with "little" things. And we can do it only through stillness and prayer. First we still our mind, moment to moment, allowing true prayer to come. True prayer is asking for vision and nothing else. Then we start experiencing a shift in our attitudes and in our perceptions. This gives us more inner strength and gives more power to our next attitudes and perceptions.

At this stage we often experience moments of great peace and moments of distress. Usually the moments of peace follow the perception of a miracle, whereas the moments of distress come when we seem to see nothing at all and to be back in the madness of the chaotic world. We seem to be deceived by God. We might then experience a feeling of being "let down" by God. This is because we still think that we are separate from God and from our brothers. This belief continues to bring with it its fruition, which is fear, guilt and pain. There we often experience the guilt of not being spiritual enough. We feel guilty of not being a "good" student. We experience a sense of failure because we still believe that we have to strive for vision. In other words, we still believe that we have to make ourselves, thus refusing to take what is referred to as the second place. This second place is the fact of being created perfect. It is the very fact of accepting God's gift to us. It is accepting our Cause or Source. This second place is only in the dream for in Heaven there is no second, no third. Yet, this place is the only way out of the dream, because the infinite Cause can only have an infinite effect, a perfect and sinless creation in the likeness of its Creator.

And now we see why we have to trust God even when we know nothing. It is only through experiencing that the unknown is the only safety, that we can truly know we are safe beyond all form and circumstance. We might know intellectually that our true safety cannot depend on a finite form or a finite circumstance, but it is only when we *experience* it that we truly know it. So it is that God has to be an experience and is, in fact, the only real experience there is. This One Experience is beyond time and space. It is eternal. We are this One Experience.

7. Why is trust the most essential step in God's perfect plan?

God's perfect plan comes from God's Will. And as it is God's Will, it knows no delay. Yet God's perfect plan has a beginning and an end, but this is only so in our *perception* of it. A perception implies time and space. A perception implies separation: a perceiver and a perceived. God's plan was set up at the "beginning", when the "unthinkable" thought of separation occurred. We can also say that God's plan is set up every time a thought of separation occurs.

This shows that God's plan can be accomplished only by the letting go of the thought of separation, the thought that we are not complete and whole now. This implies that we go beyond words and beyond belief. Words refer to concepts and concepts refer to the finite experience. This is really all that we know as separate beings. And we believe only in what we know. The "unthinkable" thought that separation is possible entails the making up of the whole world we see. The only way out of this world is then to go beyond words and beyond belief. This cannot be done through any finite form, for the finite form that would lead to it would limit infinity. This is not possible.

Now, how can we go beyond words and belief without one single form to rely on? It can only be through what the world might call madness and which is total and pure *trust*. This is love through the acceptance of what is beyond knowing intellectually. To accept what is beyond knowing intellectually implies complete trust.

Let us call to reason to show us why it has to be so. God's perfect plan is that we know Him Who is infinite perfection. Yet, all that we believe we know is finite imperfection. Trust becomes then the most essential step we have to take so that God, Perfection or reality, can *reveal* Itself to us.

God does not depend on form for His existence. He does not depend on time and space. However, we believe that we do. We do not believe in our Source. We believe that our source is ourselves. We believe that we have made ourselves out of the past and we are trying to improve ourselves in a future that does not exist. In doing so we totally "sacrifice" the present, allowing us to suffer, accepting pain and guilt through limited judgment. This is how the illusion of a chaotic world is set up.

The only way out of this illusion is perfect trust. It is essential that we understand what real trust means because if we still believe that trust is trust in some thing or some body, we merely strengthen our belief in separation, thus making ourselves weaker and weaker, ultimately bound to death. Only real trust allows our perceptions to be changed so that we become more and more aware

of love's presence, more and more grounded in a
new awareness beyond words and belief.

CHAPTER FOUR

WHAT IS WILLINGNESS AND HOW DO WE BECOME WILLING?

So it is that God's Will is so loving that, through Spirit, it reaches out into the dream of separation and uses the dream we made as a way home.

WHAT IS WILLINGNESS AND HOW DO WE BECOME WILLING?

The only reality in the universe is love. What is not love is an illusion and therefore does not exist. But we believe in the opposite of love, which is fear. And "to fear" is to fear something. What is this thing that we fear that does not exist?

Something we fear is something we do not want. And the one thing we do not want is to be unhappy. Why, then, do we feel unhappy if we do not want it?

We feel unhappy, or rather unhappiness is made real to us because we believe in it. We believe unhappiness is possible. This belief happened in time long ago when the thought of separation occurred. There is no idle thought. A thought produces an effect, which is real to the thinker. This is the one law of the universe. To be separate means to be limited to the outside of what we are separated from. Therefore, if we think we are separated from the whole universe and all our brothers, we experience a sense of total weakness and total helplessness. How does the ego react to this?

Because this feeling is highly unbearable, the ego – or the sense of separation – makes up its whole world based on suffering and guilt. Suffering is seen as a reality and guilt has to come. If we suffer it has to be *because* of somebody or something. This can be others, ourselves, or the god we made. By projecting guilt outside, we try to escape our responsibility for this, or rather our idea of responsibility. This has to be so because of our belief that we make ourselves. We want to strengthen our limits and our weakness. Our way to do this is to find guilt everywhere, as much as we can, to prove that it is not our fault and that we are "much better than that".

To prove that we are "much better than that" we *want* to be punished. A punishment is a bargain. It is an attack upon somebody to make him pay for his sins. We want to be punished to prove to ourselves that by paying the price of the punishment we are not guilty anymore.

As long as I believe that my brother is guilty, I believe he can fail and sin. Thus do I believe that I also can fail and sin. Then all my striving aims at proving that he has sinned, but that I am now "forgiven" *because* I have paid the price of unhappiness, sickness and death.

So it is that we keep reincarnating in limited bodies to pay for our failures – or sins – and thus escape the tremendous guilt that prevents us to be happy. This is an endless process that is based on the thought of separation. How can someone who sees his own destruction everywhere be happy? He constantly wants to pay any price to escape this destruction. He is willing to be sick and die to escape his death. He chooses death himself to be stronger than death. This is insane. Yet the thought of separation can only lead to this.

We are in truth totally whole and sane. This means that nothing can hurt us, though we might believe everything can. We are totally safe because we are created perfect in the likeness of our Father. Our creation holds in itself the means of escaping this mad detour into the belief in separation. This is done in time by God's plan for us, which is perfect because it is God's Will. Yet, the only thing that is asked of us for this plan to be worked out is our willingness.

1. What is God's Will or Plan for us?

God's Will is beyond time. It has to be accomplished with no delay because God, or Perfection, knows no delay. Therefore, true Will and true Accomplishment are one. A plan implies time. It supposes unfolding. A plan is set up and then worked out until it is fulfilled. A plan is connected with the world of time and space, the world of illusions or the dream.

This means that on one side we seem to have God's Will beyond time and space, perfect and already accomplished, and on the other side God's plan waiting upon time and space to be worked out. What does this mean? Reason will tell us that God cannot fail. So, in truth, God's plan and God's Will are accomplished. Still, somewhere, somehow, God's plan has to be worked out. Why?

What is God's plan? God's plan is our way home, our salvation, our way to happiness. This means vision or our awareness of Oneness. Where does this awareness come from? It has to come from God because God is all there is.

How is it then, that we can be unaware of Oneness, given the fact that God's Will knows no delay? This "impossibility" seems possible to us because we are the Son of God and God has a total and infinite respect for His Son and his *thoughts*.

There has been one "unthinkable" thought that we *seem* to have made, the thought of separation. And even this "unthinkable" thought is not opposed by God. To oppose it would be an attack from God and attack is alien to God.

Being the One Son of God, we are in truth like God, alien to attack. However we believe to be subject to attack because we believe in separation. What we believe becomes real *to us*. This is how the dream of separation is made real for us. The fact that, being one in truth, we can still dream of separation is the very proof of our infinite state of beingness as the One Son of God – that which is also called the Sonship. If God opposed our mad thoughts, God would not be real and neither would we. There would be nothing or no thing. Yet, we say "I" exist and "I" think. And even if the thoughts we believe in are not real, the very fact of thinking is a sure sign of our Source Which has never left us. In fact, God is unaware of the thought of separation because this thought is not real.

When we believe in separation, we make time and space. Because of the Sonship, which is a law that cannot be broken, the plan for the Atonement – or the recognition of oneness – is immediately set up as an effect of our thought of separation. This plan cannot fail because it is like its Source. This plan has to use time and space to undo what we have made, exactly the same way we have made it, but going backward, going home. This use of time and space by Spirit is what is often referred to as "the Word made flesh".

So it is that God's Will is so loving that, through Spirit, it reaches out into the dream of separation and uses the dream we made as a way home. But because of the Sonship, God will never force us to go home, simply because God sees us home. Then we have to be willing to let go of the dream and this is the only thing we have to "do". For if we "do" anything else, which is to keep believing in the dream, we only make more and more illusions.

God's plan, being of God, is infinite. It holds, then, infinite patience. Because it is infinite, it is perfect. For perfection and infinity are the same. This is why we will all ultimately go home, or rather we will all be aware in time of the fact that we have always been home.

*2. Do we have free choice of God's Will always –
all ways – being done?*

The answer to this question is "yes" in the dream
and "no" in truth or Heaven. Let us remember that
the dream is not a dream in itself, it is a dream for
each one of us. The dream is different for each one
of us, because as a result of an individual thought
of separation, we each make an individual dream.
Its forms and aspects vary from person to person
and the only common factor is that it is a dream
and therefore not real.

As long as we are in the dream, we have free choice
to go home. And this is merely because we can *not*
go home unless we are willing to do so. Unless we
are wholly willing to go home *because* it is our
natural state, *because* we are home in truth, we
delay *for us* our awareness of being home, which
means that delay becomes real to us.

The dream itself is very well set up in its madness.
This is because of the power of our thoughts. Every
single thought produces an effect. When we want
something, we make what we want.

Let us see now more closely what is the nature of
the dream or what happens when we want some
thing in the finite world. When we want some
thing, we believe in what we want, otherwise we
would not want it. So, whenever we want to be
happy *as a result* of a finite form – special

relationship, money, health – we make what we believe in which is the form itself *and the lack of it*. When we want some thing, we make that thing *and* its "opposite" because we believe in its opposite. When we want a special relationship, we make it somehow but we also make a lack of communication and a sense of separation. When we want money, we might make money but we also make poverty. When we want health, we might work out a temporary "healing" but we also make sickness. This is because we believe these things are real and we make them real for us. This process is often referred to as the law of karma. It comes directly from the unlimited power God has given to His Son. Yet, here we clearly see that the law of karma – or cause and effect in the world of forms – is effective *only* when we believe in it. In other words, it is effective as long as we are asleep which is as long as we believe in the need for some thing, as long as we believe the finite dream is real.

It is only in the plan that we have free choice of God's Will being done. Reason will tell us that when the plan is accomplished for us, our will and God's Will are truly recognized as one and the question of choice disappears. Then creation begins.

Still, we can delay God's plan for a very long time, but not indefinitely. The reason for this is that the dream is a finite dream. In that sense we do not really have a choice of delaying God's plan indefinitely because "indefinitely" is alien to the very nature of the finite dream. The finite ego brings with itself its own destruction. This is why we will all ultimately awaken.

Now comes the question of predestination. If God's Will is always – all ways – being done, it seems that we are predestined in time and space; whatever we might think or do, we appear to have no choice and to be lead somewhere, somehow, exactly and perfectly, according to the plan. Do we then really play a role in the universal perfection?

This is a matter of identity. If we identify with a body, we experience time, space, delay, suffering and death. Then failure is real *to us*. Then we experience the illusion of delaying God's plan and God *cannot interfere with this* for it is not real for God. Do we understand this? No, as long as we are in time. Still we can be willing to understand it and this will be enough to lead us out of this "unanswerable" question.

Yet we can use words here that will show us the way out of this. Delay in itself is an illusion. In truth, there is no delay because there is no time. Still we believe there is a past and a future, thus preventing us from being aware of the infinity of the present or the ever-creating beingness. In our belief of limitations, we make a past which is no longer there because it is limited, and a future which is not yet here for the same reason. This is why we cannot experience the fullness of the present. Moreover, as present can only be experienced fully or not at all, we are not at all aware of the present.

What then is our role in the universal perfection? Just to be aware of perfection. Nothing more, but nothing less. Perfection is reality. And our awareness of reality is total or it is not. The only way to this awareness is a pure willingness. A willingness for reality to reveal itself, a total giving up of all private thoughts we ever had or will have. A willingness to see reality *because it is real.*

3. How can I be willing?

To be willing, I have to be open and trust. If I shut myself from my brothers or from God, I deny them something that I want only for myself. This has to be because I think that I can get "something" only by somebody else losing that "something". I believe in a finite quantity of forms and not in the unlimited power of the One Mind. If I believe in the past, which by essence is limited because it has given me limited things, I want things from the past either to re-occur the same way or to happen in the future in a different way. In both cases it has to be *my* way because I believe my happiness would come from what I have taught myself, from what I know from my own learning.

The thinking of the world always requires that I have to do something in order to acquire something. This something that I want takes many forms but it is always ultimately a state of peace and happiness. If I want peace, I have to strive and struggle and battle to get it. If I want happiness, I have to "deserve" it by doing something. And if I do not feel at peace and happy, I feel guilty or project guilt on others. This is the endless struggle of the ego.

On my way home, when I have started the journey back to infinity, there is a "frightening" thought that might seem to stop me on the way. This thought is the fear that my individual identity will be lost. This has to be because of the nature of my individual identity. It is based on differences. So when I catch a glimpse of what could be my true identity – total oneness with the whole universe – I see that all that I believed and which made my "self" will disappear and vanish. This is hardly bearable. How then could I be willing in such a state? This is impossible as long as I am not aware somehow, somewhere, of the presence of love, as long as I am not aware of experiencing something different, something entirely new and unknown. And I have to experience joy and happiness through this something. How can this be done?

It can be done only by sitting quietly and really looking at things whatever the "cost" may be. This has to come gradually in the measure of my shift in valuing the things I might think I will lose. If I value the body as an end, I cannot be willing. But if I begin to trust the unknown through my experience of it, I am willing. This is enough, for my goal has been set and the opportunities to be more and more willing are constantly provided to me.

The willingness itself is in me. How could I be willing to be taught and experience something entirely different and new if I did not trust? And if I trust it is because there is "something" in me that tells me that I cannot be deceived. How can I believe that what I hear is true unless I already know it or I remember, however vaguely, having experienced it?

This is obviously telling me that an individual identity does not exist in truth. The more I realize this, the more I experience joy, peace and happiness. Then, and only then, do I begin to see that only a universal experience is real and necessary – necessary in the sense that it cannot not be.

4. What is true willingness?

True willingness is whole or it is not. It can only come through happiness. Yet happiness itself has to come from willingness, because cause and effect are one and not separated. Now, how is it that I can experience happiness even if I am not aware of being willing? I can do so *only* because willingness is already in me as the Son of God. This is the very proof of my belonging to the divine Sonship. Divine Sonship means divine nature or infinite nature.

If I were not infinite being, I could not think of infinity. There is "something" there that might be temporarily hidden but which is the only real part in me. Still I might seem to be filled with individual thought forms. I have to understand that these forms are not real and they merely seem to keep me from my Source or What I am.

If we want to realize what true willingness is, we have to understand what is "untrue" willingness. Untrue willingness is to want something in the form. Then we might say: "I am willing to be healed", meaning "I want this form of disease to go away." We might get a result there, but it would be an illusion for only the form or the symptom would have disappeared but not the source of the disease itself.

We then begin to see that only true willingness can

be effective, a willingness that is totally pure, totally beyond any desire for any form to go, stay or come. True willingness can only be experienced in a holy instant, in this instant where the mind is totally still and the heart open to the truth because it is the truth. True willingness is then to be totally open.

Then might come the thought: "If this is so, there is no hope for me because true willingness seems very far away indeed on my way home". This is true only in the illusion, therefore it is not true. It is only our perception of limits that makes limits real to us. True willingness *is* within us.

There again we see that with all we "know", we cannot of ourselves change our perceptions, and we have to let them be changed by Him who knows of infinity. Here we clearly see the function of Spirit or the One Who knows of infinity, the One Teacher Who is aware of our dream as a dream. Here we see that anyone who has achieved pure willingness is consciously aware of Oneness, and being *consciously* unlimited, he has saved the world. Then, and only then, can he truly say to you: "I am your way home".

Now, how has he achieved pure willingness? He has achieved it by doing nothing and truly not mixing up willingness and readiness. He has truly said: "I of my own self can do nothing". He has given up every private thought he ever had. He has "died" to the known in one perfect instant. He has been truly willing for the truth to reveal itself. He has once and for all not interfered at all. He has been totally transparent. And because this pure willingness has allowed knowledge to be truly seen, the grounds for personal identification have disappeared. Oneness with the One Infinite Thought of the universe is remembered. Time has vanished and the world is saved. The very fact that time is needed for some thing is now irrelevant. Only that remains which truly exists: omnipresence, omniscience, omnipotence, in other words, reality.

5. Am I a puppet in a world of illusion?

If I ask this question, it is because I believe in the world of illusion. What is this world made of? It is an effect of finite thoughts. These thoughts are private. They reflect the belief of "striving for something". It must be clearly understood that the source of this world of illusion is nowhere else. As long as I believe that I have to strive to get something, I literally make myself little, weak and wanting something or some things. I make my world of chaos. I make the law of this world, which is "seek but do not find".

"Seek" because you want something you do not have. And "do not find" because every time you seem to find it, you admit that there is something outside of you which you value and which you lack *because* it is outside. You make real the "fact" that you do not have it and you keep trying and trying to be complete by acquiring "things" and "bodies" in an endless and desperate search. The more you have the illusion to possess more things and more bodies, the more there is to acquire, and you end up in hell.

When we see this we begin to understand what it is to be out of control or a puppet in a world of illusion. To have control is to be the king, or the queen, to be totally safe and keep things in proper order. Now what proper order can there be in a world of illusion? Who is to come first? Either it is me and I get attacked and killed by the anger of my brothers or the god I made, or it is somebody else who has total power over me. In both cases fear is unbearable and guilt inevitable. Fear of pain and guilt comes from the deep failure I see in myself.

With this sight, I can be nothing but a puppet. The situation has no way out and my fear can only increase. The more I strive for something, the more I realize that it does not bring me happiness. Still, as I believe in this world of illusion, I strive more and more. And above all I do not want to see my helplessness. This is why I may react violently to anyone who would dare to show it to me. I do not want to see any way out because I believe that it is there and only there that I can be happy.

Then, I carefully plan to acquire wealth, fame, health or relationships. I thoroughly plan my attack in all directions. I strive hard to make something of myself because above all I do not want to see that I am only making myself this puppet in a world of illusion. I am now totally out of control, but I carefully attack everywhere to make sure that getting something will bring me happiness. I am making hell real for myself.

Now this seems a frightening picture and it is one indeed. But unless I see this process of illusions based on illusion, I cannot escape this world. I have to face this process and cease to hide it in darkness. I have to bring out in the light its cornerstone: the belief in separation, the belief finite things are real, the belief the body is valuable for what it offers, the belief I have to strive or to do some thing to find happiness.

In other words I must be willing to turn within and ask Him Who created me for His perfect Will to be shown to me. I have to be willing to receive His gift that His Spirit has kept safe for me. I have to be willing for Spirit or my Self to show me that being a puppet in a world of illusion is nothing but an illusion. I have to be willing for my real mind to show me that my will and goals are aligned with God's.

6. How do I know when my will or goals are aligned with God's?

My will or goals are not aligned with God's when I listen to my limited self, when I try with my separate mind to understand something. I have to admit that it is impossible to grasp anything with a finite mind.

The only way is to still my mind and go to silence. God's Voice is heard in silence and stillness only. To understand this, I have to experience it. So whenever the question arises how to know when my will or goals are aligned with God's, I can be sure that I am not still and silent.

Now, how can I become still and silent? Only by being truly willing to know what my true goals are. I must look at what I want and decide what I *really* want. Do I want total peace or do I want a special "form" of peace? Do I want total happiness or a special "form" of happiness? I have to realize that a special "form" of peace or happiness is merely the belief that a finite form outside will bring an effect of peace or happiness inside. This is impossible because the belief in the necessity of a finite form brings with it its opposite, which is the lack of it. Only when I realize that all that I have taught myself, all that I have learned has failed to bring me true happiness, only then do I really want to turn within and ask for total inner guidance.

In the process of learning, I often turn within to ask for a "limited" guidance. Somewhere, somehow I know that my true goals are aligned with God's, but I still believe in some special form of happiness. I then turn within and ask for a limited guidance – which of these two possibilities shall I choose? – thus excluding all the others.

The term "inner guidance" is actually very specific and excludes "outer guidance". Outer guidance is the guidance of the world or rather the guidance of a form. It can even be what we call a "good" guidance, a friend, a relative, somebody with "good" intents for us, somebody we perceive as asking us to do something in order to get something for our "good".

Does this mean that I should not listen to any "external" advice? If I realize that all events and circumstances are set for my own best interest, then I understand that when I ask "what shall I do?" it must be clear to me that my asking is meaningful only in the measure of my certainty that God cannot deceive me. So it is that I become more and more certain that my goals are aligned with God's *because* it is God's Will that it be so. And my only asking is rather: "show me Your Will which is mine". This itself soon shifts to "I am willing to see Your Will in this." There a statement has replaced the demand. This statement is real only if we really know that God's Will is our happiness and that God's Will does not wait upon time to be fulfilled. Then we have fully accepted that there is no order of difficulty in miracles. There indeed are we aware of being a miracle, which is the recognition of truth.

Thus do we find ourselves totally at peace because we do know truly that our will and our goals are aligned with God's. Our goals have been truly set. We know that the inner guidance can never fail and we merely behold its outer form in a constant miracle. Any event, situation or circumstance becomes meaningful and merely bears witness to God's plan.

7. When do I take action and when should I wait?

For the world's thinking to take action is to do something, whereas to wait is to not do something for a certain time. The world is always asking when is the right time but the answer is never certain. To the real world, taking action and waiting are the same because waiting is an action. They are just different movements in form. And what happens in form is nothing but an effect of thought. Right thinking leads either to right action or right waiting without any striving or concern. We can never truly know of ourselves what is the right thing to do, and the only way to know it is to ask Him Who knows. This is done through inner listening. What we hear then is in the measure of our certainty that the Voice for God cannot fail to speak to us. It is also in the measure of our awareness of our true identity, which entails trust. The more we trust, the more we know what to do and when. There is no other thing to do than to listen and trust.

It might happen that we experience fear in a situation that seems to demand an urgent answer. There we might go through experiencing a "temporary lack of an answer". With honest practice, we will realize that the answer is always perfect in its form and in its time. We will understand that we have never missed anything, we have never made a real mistake and we have never been too late. Understanding this, we become more and more faithful and we realize that we hardly go through this kind of experience anymore, or rather this kind of experience does not seem to affect us anymore. We gradually experience a sense of rightful movement and this sense becomes more and more permanent.

Then we truly see ourselves moving towards inner happiness and peace. Whatever the world might seem to say or do to us, we are not affected. We feel surely grounded in a safety that cannot flicker. And we just watch the fruition of this state. Harmony and peace extend all around us. Miracles blossom everywhere. We move in a totally peaceful state because the perfection of God's plan has become real to us.

CHAPTER FIVE

WHY HAS THE TIME COME FOR FEAR TO CEASE?

Reality, which we are, is eternal and whole now.

WHY HAS THE TIME COME FOR FEAR TO CEASE?

Fear in itself is an illusion. Yet, we do not believe it is so. We think there is nothing more real than fear and this is why we experience it. We see it everywhere because of our whole belief system, which is based on fear. What is fear?

Fear is the belief that something might happen to us bringing pain and sorrow. We believe from our own judgment over the past that pain and sorrow are everywhere. We also believe that moments of joy and happiness can occur because we have these remembrances of such a state. Yet, we believe that we cannot have total control over the future and we fear the future. And we do this because we believe in the reality of the past. We have taught ourselves that we feel happy or unhappy according to the kind of event that we go through. We believe that our happiness depends on forms over which we have hardly any control.

Who can prevent a natural catastrophe? Who can prevent a sudden assault? Who can have control over the behavior of others? Who can add a few inches to his height? Apparently we are totally tied up by everything. There is no real safety in the world we see. It seems that our happiness can be threatened by everything. Fear has come for us.

Yet, we have been told for many centuries not to fear. But many of us do not seem convinced. However, this time is the time for fear to cease. It is a time for peace and love to be openly felt and shared. Why is it so? What do we have to do for this? What happens to us when we fear no more?

1. What is it that causes us the most fear?

When we look at the way we fear, we realize there are degrees of fear. Some fears are not unbearable, some are. Yet, the most frightful thought that we can have is the loss of personal identity. For many of us this seems of no concern. It is so because of the complicated way the ego has built its belief system. Yet we must realize that all this belief system relies on the belief in personal identity and the ego is terrified by the thought of losing it. What is a personal identity?

A personal identity is made up of characteristics that belong only to the person having this identity. This identity is private property. It is something that makes "us" and without it, we are not "us". Now, what do we know about us? Nothing but our past. We seem to have made ourselves since we were born through a certain number of circumstances. Even if we believe in reincarnation, it is the same process. "We" reincarnate to "improve" ourselves, to pay for our debts and to strive to be "better". Above all else we do not want to disappear as a body. Why?

This is because disappearing as a body contradicts totally what we believe in, which is the fact of being a body and nothing but a body. Yet we truly know that we *are*. We exist. We are real. What we see disappearing is only "our" body. Reason will tell us that if we are not this body, the fear of disappearing will vanish when we know who we truly are. This seems very simple. Yet, one of the things we fear most is to know who we are. Why?

Our "happiness" and our "safety" are presently based on *not* knowing who we are. Knowing who we are is seeing who we are. And we constantly refuse to see who we are because what we see *with* our belief in separation is frightful. If we carefully and honestly look at ourselves, we see weakness, total helplessness and despair. We see a puppet in a world of chaos.

When we face what we are as a body, we see that death will come ultimately and we will lose this body, which is our identity. The body is for us the symbol of safety or, at least, of hope. We believe that as long as there is life in this body there is hope. Death is really this ultimate step that we refuse by all means. The whole behavior of the world is based on this. Death is hidden, as ugly and unbearable. It is forbidden to speak about it. It is the symbol of sadness. It is something that is constantly there with its terrible threat and which has to happen to others, but not to us.

The body is so valuable to us that we often build theories "proving" that the body will survive death. The idea of being Spirit is so alien to our thought system that we cannot imagine ourselves without this form that we call a body. We accept the fact that God is not in a body, but not us! We strive with our finite mind to find a way out of this, and we make up an immortal body. What is an immortal body?

It is a body that has an immortal future, a future that will never end. It is a form that we take out of the past and project into the future to be sure not to die. This process is perfectly natural to the mind which believes in separation, because it is the only way to "ensure a good future". We fear the future, yet the future is not real because it is not *now*. It does not exist.

Thus we are constantly in a process of imagining something to come that has no reality *now* and therefore does not exist. This process never brings real peace because real peace is now. This process is based on the denial of the now. It constantly refuses to see what is now, because what is seen "now" is a projection of chaos and imperfection related either to memories about an imagined past or to expectations about an imagined future. This is why the physical eyes are made not to see what is real. They are made to look outside, to look more and more at things which are not us. Thus we are desperately striving to find peace and happiness through forms which we are not. This is how we constantly deny our being to ourselves, trying to make up a future, which can only be an illusion, *because* reality can *not* change and therefore does not know of any future. Reality, which we are, is eternal and whole *now*.

2. Why is it the human state to fear?

The human state comes from the belief in separation. To be separate means to be apart from "something" and to have an identity that is different from that "something". The cause of separation is a mistake, a reflection upon oneself, a thought of being a separate entity. It is a thought of being something which contradicts itself: being and being apart from being. Being is infinite and now, or it is not. So it is that being is being everything or nothing. Being cannot be nothing. I know this because I say "I".   Something, somewhere, somehow says "I". Then I know that being *is*. What truly says "I" cannot be nothing. "I" live, "I" exist. What can be the cause of this "I" if not "I" itself?

My reflection upon myself and my struggling is the sign of a contradiction. What is this contradiction? A contradiction is the acceptance of two premises that exclude one another. Here the two premises are: First, I say "I", meaning "I am". Second, I believe I am a body, knowing that a body dies. I believe in death. So it is that the human state is to believe in life and death at the same time. It is to believe that happiness and unhappiness are possible. The human state believes in opposites. It believes in good *and* evil.

What is good and evil? We call evil that which we do not want because we fear it, because we think it will bring pain and sorrow. We call good that which we want because we think it will bring us happiness.

The belief in good and evil is the belief that a finite form, which is an effect of the thought of separation, is the *cause* of our happiness or unhappiness. It is a mistake, it is the thought of separation itself. The belief in good and evil makes our human state, thus shutting ourselves out of Heaven – or our awareness of being one with God or Perfection.

We are in a human state because we believe the body has a value of its own. This is why we reincarnate. As a consequence we fear more and more because we strive to acquire outside of us all that never brings us real peace of mind.

What is the remedy for all this? It is not to get rid of the body because the body is the effect of a thought. The remedy is to have this thought corrected so that we clearly see the contradiction we have believed in. Our belief system is built according to what we perceive. The human state entails a perceiver and a perceived. In other words: separation. As long as there is perception, the perceiver is not the perceived. And as the perceiver understands more and more that he has no control over the perceived, he fears more and more and attacks everywhere and everyone including himself. His desires totally conflict. He wants peace by attacking and he wants happiness by accepting unhappiness. He uses the tools that make hell to make Heaven. And he has only one way out of this chaos: to be aware of his true state of beingness.

3. Why must we become aware of our true state of beingness?

We are in a state of beingness because we are not a body but Spirit. As long as we deny this state, we literally refuse to see. What is it that we should see?

If we are Spirit, we should be able to see manifestations of this Spirit. And if we do not see them, it must be because we do not see correctly. This is because we do not look correctly. We look for something that is not there. We look for a result of our striving. We believe *we* have to make ourselves, to strive to do things. Then we constantly judge what *we* do to see if it is good or bad.

The truth is that we never do anything. When we say that we do something, the "we" we refer to is not real. In truth the work is done by Spirit at work. We have the illusion that we achieve something by ourselves. Then we feel "better". We even think that we can improve our behavior and become more "spiritual". We do not see that by striving we turn away from the real cause of the work which is done. We fight to succeed in the world, even if we call this world and our work spiritual. We might succeed after a very, very long time of struggle, many lifetimes, because of our goal that is more and more firmly established. Yet we can save a great deal of time by choosing *now* to perceive correctly.

If we really are in a state of beingness, nothing can threaten us. We cannot fail. When we really believe this, we simply let perfection achieve its work in time. This work seems to take time because it deals with the undoing of the belief in time. It deals with the belief in humanness. It is only because of this belief that we experience a sense of time. To experience a sense of time is merely not being present, it is believing in the reality of the past and the future which are not here *now*.

As long as we believe that we have to *do* something, we believe that the future has to be better than now. And we cannot see the perfection of now. What is "doing"? Doing is achieving something. As long as we think something has to be achieved, we deny the perfection of reality which is now. We do not see that God simply *is* and that we are a perfect creation, a full and whole extension of God encompassing everything.

To create is not to do something. To create is to extend. To do is to project outside. We have to understand that there is no outside. Outside is an illusion or nothingness. So it is that doing and being contradict. God does not do anything and as the one perfect Son of God, we do not do anything. When we truly and fully grasp this, we are back to our true state, which is being and creating eternally, perfectly one with God. Then, and only then, in this state beyond time, are we back home where we have always been.

Now comes the question: why do we speak of Spirit being at work, which seems to mean that Spirit is doing something? This is truly an illusion. Yet, as long as we believe we exist in time, seeing the perfection of this work is necessary *for* us to begin to experience more and more a sense of our true state, which is perfect peace. First, reason tells us that it cannot be otherwise, and then we experience it gradually throughout an illusion of time. This is how our way home seems to happen in time and space. In truth it already happened at the moment of separation. This journey home is a process of undoing what has been done. The fact that it has to be led by the perfection of Spirit is the only way to understand that what we have made cannot take us home. So it is that this "journey" home takes exactly the same way we took to go away from home, but backwards.

On the way home miracles appear more and more frequently and shorten time *for* us, until the "time" has come for God to take the last step for us. The fact that this last step has to be taken is an illusion. Yet this illusion, through Spirit's guidance, serves a purpose, which is to be seen as an illusion. He who sees the dream as a dream has to be awake.

4. Has the time come for fear to cease?

In this dream of time we see degrees or levels. What are these levels? They are our levels of consciousness. We gradually shift from level to level, thus being led from the nightmare to the happy dream. The dream itself is highly individualized, yet, while in the dream, we constantly share. What do we share?

What we constantly share is thought. Some of us are not aware of this and still have the illusion to share forms like words, money, physical presence, joining with bodies. This is not sharing; it is merely acquiring nothing and losing nothing at the same time. Yet, it is perfectly used by Spirit to show us that it is nothing.

What we truly share is teaching what we learn and learning what we teach at the same time. We teach what we believe in and our level of consciousness entails what we teach through what we learn. As our level of consciousness is shifting now to a deeper awareness of love's presence, this awareness is shared at the same time and bears fruit.

So it is that today, with the opening of the third millennium, the time has come for fear to cease in the dream of time. This is because for centuries we have mostly shared thoughts of fear, beliefs in sin, sacrifice and death, but this is not so any more.

When we did this, we kept each other in the illusion of a chaotic world. We made this illusion real for us, we taught it, and we experienced it. It was a difficult time. The One Thought of Oneness and infinite Love was so alien to our belief system that it took us a long time to catch a glimpse of the true meaning of being children of God. Many times we lost the way. We often "punished" those who were led to stand up to remind us of Love and Perfection. We strongly refused to accept the gift of God because of our guilt. We were teaching a fundamental contradiction: Infinite perfection, Love or God, punishes itself!

If we look around us today, we see that more and more of us are going beyond words. Many of us are now in the happy dream. We are more openly teachers of God. This awareness of living a happy dream is shared, as was shared the awareness of living a nightmare. This is why, by being aware of our true infinite state of love, we are truly helpful. Through this awareness we share true loving thoughts. And these loving thoughts allow us and others to see miracles and harmony everywhere. This is how we merely watch healing take place everywhere as we watch our own healing.

What we see is the sharing process at work. We see its fruition and it brings great joy. Many of us today are aware of a quickening of the work of Spirit. This is an effect of the fact that our level of consciousness is changing. More of us are willing to see the truth above all else. We are more willing to let go of our illusions about our limited human state and to let the last illusion of forgiveness show us *through* forgiveness that there is nothing to forgive. The time has now come for fear to cease.

5. *How can I cease to fear?*

Here you might come to me and say: "This might be true, but I do not see my state of beingness. It seems far away and unattainable. Maybe some of us are aware of it, but not me. What should I do now to cease to fear?"

What you have to do is not to do anything particular but just watch your world, that world which surrounds you. Do not turn away from it. Face it whatever the cost might seem to be. It is the only way to discover that there is no cost. You might not want to truly look at it and question it because you might have been told that it is a sin to ask a question. Would God hide anything from you? Would God not answer His beloved son? Whom would you trust, God Who is loving you infinitely or theories made by finite minds? Do you really want to know of God's gift to you? Does this gift have limits? And where can it be if not everywhere?

So begin with what you think you have: your world. Observe it carefully. See how it is made. Do not be satisfied with theories you do not understand. Do not strive with your mind. Just watch and see what this world shows you. It is only by looking at it that you can understand it is insane and chaotic. You will clearly see its madness and you will stop believing it can bring something valuable of itself.

By really watching without "ready made" concepts you cannot fail to begin to see Spirit at work in your life. What happens when you merely watch? You simply do not judge. You become non-judgmental. This attitude is essential to see Spirit in your life because Spirit itself is non-judgmental, or rather Spirit merely judges everything as perfect.

You see what you want to see. If you want to see what is not there, you see it. If you want to see what is truly there, you see it. Spirit is constantly offering you the opportunity to recognize what is now. What is now has no memory. A newborn child does not judge. He opens his eyes and watches without any judgment.

Now go and survey your past and see what you have built up through it. See what you now believe in because you have been constantly judging. You were told to judge *because* it was the only means of finding a seeming security. You have been told to protect yourself, to attack in order to defend yourself. You have been told you were the weakest person there is. You have been told to make something of yourself, even spiritually. Is this the Son of God? Is this infinite power ever given to His Son? Is this perfect peace?

Yes, indeed, either this world is real and God is a man-made projection, or God is real and this world is a mistake that merely needs correction. It is not a mistake in itself, it is nothing. What is a mistake is the way you see it. The world you see is not real. The real world you do not see.

Now you begin to see that this *must* be true. Yet, in order for you to see it truly, and for it to be real to you, you have to experience it. What do you have to do to experience what you are? Nothing, but be willing. You must be willing now. To be willing is to practice that which your Self tells you "Listen to my word and put it into practice". This means: you are given the words that show you the way, and it is only by trusting the way that the way brings you home. Now it is time for you to be willing to trust. Be patient and watch. Your goal is high, much higher than you can imagine. Yet the power in you is infinite for it was given you when you were created. This seems to have happened a long time ago. In truth it is happening now, for only now is eternal, or rather it *is* now, for in eternity nothing happens, everything merely is.

6. What does God want us to do?

God does not want us to do anything because God is unaware of the world we made. God is only aware of reality, being Reality Itself. Can reality be aware of something that is not real? God really wants us to be happy. As the Will of God knows no delay, we are truly happy, though we might not be aware of being happy. God is loving, eternally and infinitely. Love is ever creating like Itself. This state of endless creation is perfect happiness and perfect peace. God is perfectly at peace forever because God is only aware of peace. God's Will is truly accomplished and so is ours because God's Will and ours are one. Yet there is still something to be done. What is this that has to be done, given the fact that we do not have to do anything?

What has to be done is to let go of our belief system. To let go is not to take action. It is merely to still our mind and let whatever comes come. To still our mind needs training. But we must realize that this training is never striving. It is a constant vigilance, a constant remembrance of our goal of peace. We do not attain peace through striving. Striving is some sort of suffering and suffering is not necessary. Why?

This is because of our goal, which is the attainment of peace or going back home where we already are. It is essential to understand that we *are* home. The way home is merely a succession of recognitions of our true state. It takes time in time, but it goes nowhere and it is a journey without distance. It is a journey that is already accomplished. As soon as it begins it ends. Why?

This is because this journey needs our willingness and nothing else. As soon as we are willing to begin the journey, we are willing to let Spirit guide us. Spirit is perfection. Its work seems to last for some time only because of our belief in time. Like all our beliefs, time is used for our way home. In truth, the journey itself is an illusion. It is not necessary for us, yet it is necessary for our *awareness* of our happiness.

Why do we believe that suffering is necessary? It is because we believe in separation and we believe in the reality of sin. We think: "We have not been kind to God Who has been so kind to us". God is not aware of any "unkindness" because unkindness does not exist. So it is time now to let go of the idea that suffering is necessary, that we have to pay a price for our "sins".

Let us once and for all begin with the core of all true teaching: God's Son is sinless and in his innocence lies his salvation. This means that when we recognize that we are guiltless, we are saved. What is it that we are saved from? We are saved from all illusions and their cause which is the thought of separation.

7. What comes to us when we cease to fear?

In truth nothing has come to us because we are all there is and all there is *is* total peace. Yet we are not aware of peace. Where is peace? Peace is within us and not outside. So it is that when we cease to fear, we become *aware* of the peace that is already within us. And we might say: peace has come to me. Actually, we only become aware of true inner peace, which is there already.

Why do we say *true* inner peace? The word "true" is essential. It means that this peace is real and therefore does not depend on external circumstances. It is the peace that nobody and nothing can take away from us.

The reason why we have to look inside us and nowhere else to find peace is because peace is nowhere else. How can we look inside? To know how to look inside, we must understand what "inside" means. Inside means our real mind. It is not the mind we made by projecting the thought of separation in a world outside, thus believing that we are a body separated from the world we made. If we look for peace outside in the world, we will not find peace because it is not there. When we do this, we want peace to come as an effect of separated forms and bodies that are not real. Then, this peace cannot be real. It cannot last. It might seem to last for a while but war has to come.

Why?

War has to come because we believe war is real. We believe we have to protect ourselves from war and attack. We make them both real for us and thus do we experience them. So it is that anything we do to "impose" peace on earth brings war sooner or later. Peace is inside each one of us and it is by recognizing it where it is that we allow it to manifest itself in the world. This world, then, remains a dream but it is a happy dream. What is this happy dream?

It is the total integration of human and being aspects. How is this done? It is done only by the full realization that you need do nothing. When this happens, the body has become meaningless to you. You still see it, but it is no more an obstacle to peace. You see its perfect place in time. You see at last its perfect place *now*. You merely watch it being perfectly used by Spirit. You are no longer concerned with where it goes and what it does or says, and you gently lay it aside when it is no more useful. You simply watch its perfect usefulness as a tool for learning; you watch the perfect integration of the human and being aspects. You are at peace in the happy dream.

Then you experience love and fullness beyond words and beyond belief. Because you have been truly willing to do nothing in one instant, you have gone beyond the use of words and beyond any belief. Knowledge has come to you at last, or rather you remember love and fullness *as* you. Your vision shows you that it is only by doing nothing that everything is being done. The miracle of Atonement has happened for you and everyone through your willingness to let it happen.

CHAPTER SIX

WHAT STEPS CAN A TRUE MIRACLE WORKER TAKE?

"Everyone I see is perfect".
Whenever I meet or talk to someone, I will say
silently:
"I see only perfection in you."

WHAT STEPS CAN A TRUE MIRACLE WORKER TAKE?

A miracle is a shift in perception. It is a true recognition of what is. It entails that somewhere there is a state of non-recognition and, suddenly, that state changes into a state of recognition. A miracle is the effect of a healing. A healing implies that somewhere, something is not healed. This means that this something has gone wrong. What can go wrong?

In truth or in reality, nothing. For in truth everything is perfect. "Nothing real can be threatened" means that nothing real can go wrong. What goes wrong is something that is not real. It is something that does not exist. Yet, here I am, speaking about something that has gone wrong. I must then admit that I speak about an illusion. I speak about something that has gone wrong and yet does not exist.

Then why do I speak about it? This has to be for one of the two following reasons: Either I believe that something has really gone wrong and I want to do something about it because what has gone wrong appears to bring pain; or I do not believe in it, but someone asks me to speak about it because he believes something has gone wrong and asks me the reason why.

Now, is there a reason for something that does not exist to go wrong? No, because what has gone wrong is nothingness. Yet, because of the belief in what does not exist, it is necessary *within* this belief to use words to show the way out of the belief. This way out seems to last for a while. It seems to go step by step. It appears to be a succession of recognitions of what is real, a way where miracles are milestones.

The way out of the belief in separation is our way home. It is our way towards our real state. On this way miracles are performed according to our shifts in perception. The Source of all miracles is love, and we are one with this Source. Miracles arise from our recognition of our Source. As love is beyond time, all miracles have already happened. What we merely do on our way home is to recognize in time what has already happened in truth, until we finally recognize the "last" miracle to be seen, the miracle of Atonement.

1. Are steps really necessary?

Our goal – or destination – is the recognition of the real world. The real world is beyond time. To see ourselves in the real world is to see everyone there with us. In this state of awareness, the idea of steps is irrelevant. The question is not even asked.

Yet, as long as we are in the illusion, steps are necessary because of our belief in time. These steps use time and it is the only usefulness of time. What are these steps?

The concept of steps implies a progression. For the world of illusion, somebody makes progress when he acquires some learning, some skill. He "makes" up himself by acquiring, step by step, some kind of "strength" that will enable him to defend himself against attacks: poverty, loneliness, sickness and somehow death. Thus does he prepare himself to attack. By doing this, he gives more and more power to the world which surrounds him, and he thinks he has found shelter in the "self-made man" he has become. The thing for which he strives most is to *not* look at death. And if he looks at it, it is only to make all attempts to keep it far away from himself and "delay" it as much as possible.

When we embark on our way home, we also go step by step. But this time we go backwards. We merely unlearn what we have learned. This does not mean we unlearn the skills we have been given. It means we unlearn what the world has taught us which is the belief that we have to fight to acquire something.

When we begin to face this world of illusion, we begin to understand that we do not do anything, we merely are. This recognition takes steps in time. This recognition is done through miracles. We become more and more aware of Him Who is truly at work. We are asked to participate in this work but we must not forget our sole function which is to be willing for the perfect work to be done *through* us. This is why we do not really help and no one heals anyone. We merely watch healings take place in time. Yet, these healings need us to occur in time. They need our willingness. And to be willing is the only step there is, though our state of willingness appears to be more permanent step by step.

2. How can I help?

Here I am, wanting to help. To be truly helpful I have to realize whom I want to help. I want to help my brother and myself. I want to help us to be happy. Yet, as long as I see my brother needing something, I see myself in need of something. I can only truly see my brother either giving love or calling for love. Whether he gives love or calls for love, it is because he is love himself, for only love can give love or call for love. To be love means to be real and what is real cannot be threatened.

So it is that I have to realize that my brother is perfection and *does not need anything*. This is the only way I can answer his call for love with love. This is the only way I can be truly helpful. This happens when I realize that I do not have to do anything but just be. By just being, I set the tone for Spirit to come manifesting. I cease to interfere with God's perfect plan being worked out in time.

To let Spirit come implies total trust. I can only trust totally when I cease to think that I of my own self can do something. It is then and only then that my total willingness allows Spirit to manifest itself in this world, I allow at last the Word – or Love – to be made flesh *through* me. This means that whoever sees me truly sees the Father who sent me.

This is all that we are called to do through our

willingness and our true realization that we need do nothing. Then we have total faith in Him Who does the work. Through this faith, we cannot fail to truly represent Him Who sent us. He has sent each one of us exactly where we are to be an example, to demonstrate that by *not* worrying about what to do or what to say, perfect action is undertaken by us and those around us.

We teach what we believe in, and others learn what we teach as well as we learn from others what they teach. So it is up to me to decide what I want to learn from my brother who has been sent to me. Shall I see him wanting, weak and attacking? Or shall I be willing to see what he truly is: perfection and love? The way I want to see him entails what he will teach me. And what he teaches me I will teach. My brother is truly my savior in that sense, and when I realize through my recognition of his total love that I am saved, then he cannot fail to recognize his total peace in me.

How can I recognize that my brother is total love? I can only do this by blessing him, by offering him silently all love and by asking Spirit in me to show me my brother's perfection. When I do this, I totally cease to judge him and I allow my experience of love to come. This experience brings me an awareness of what love is. It brings me a deep sense of peace, happiness and true sharing.

Then I begin to understand what true sharing

means because I see others learn by "my" example. Yet, it is not "my" private example but rather the sense of love that is felt by others *through* me. Sooner or later my brother cannot fail to recognize his total peace through me, as I was able to recognize mine through him. This is how my brother and I are saved *together*.

Each relationship I have with a brother is an opportunity for me and for him to be saved together. What I have to understand is that I must not ask for anything from him. I must not want him to change his behavior in any way because if I do this I deny him perfection. What matters *for me* in a relationship is to let it be holy −or fully loving − *through* my own willingness and *not* his. This is how we truly teach love and nothing else. This is the only way to be truly helpful.

3. How can I radiate inner peace and love all ways, always?

Given the fact that I of my own self can do nothing, who is the only One radiating inner peace and love all ways always through me? It is God and me as one. This we have to realize for our salvation. How can we realize it if not by constantly keeping a God focus?

To keep a God focus implies total trust. Would God deceive His Son? To be aware of God is the most natural thing there is *because* God has totally given Himself to us. We are not aware of this because of the thought of separation. This unbelievable belief has slipped into our mind and has built up the dream of a whole universe of chaos. To escape the dream, I have to be aware of the dream. I have to look at it, to face it and to throw away all guilt by questioning this dream.

How can I throw away this guilt to which I seem to be attracted? Only by understanding why I am attracted to it, why I want this guilt to feel safe among this insane world. I have to admit that out of my past, out of *my* learning, there is no way out. I have to stop trying to build up another illusion. What is this other illusion I keep building up?

It is a new separation. It is a new belief that I of my own self can do something. I am frantically searching to do something out of this total weakness and nothingness. I have to understand that I am not this speck of dust which is my body. I have to take the second place, which is that of a perfect creation given all there is by its perfect Creator. I have to accept the gift of God once and for all.

Then and only then do I radiate inner peace and love. And this time I understand that I do not do this *my* way, which is a separate way. But I do it all ways, for God is doing it through me. And what God does is always all ways.

Being aware of my true identity, I begin to openly respond to the love of God. I begin to be openly active in channeling peace and love. Where is *my* limit in this? If I have been *totally* open, willing, and trusting in one single instant, the whole world is saved through me. This means: the thought of separation is no more an obstacle to infinite peace and love and joy.

When I understand the one principle of this which is total love, my journey has truly begun. On this journey I just watch the perfection of the plan unfolding. I just see all my experiences as a call to trust, to be open and willing. Then, the steps become easier. I sometimes flicker, but it does not last long. I even like these moments for I begin to see them as a new opportunity to learn where my unlimited strength lies.

A miracle is an answer to the call of God. In this world where answers and miracles are needed, peace and love have to radiate through individuals. And the dream will seem to be endless if no individual is willing to trust. This is my part in God's plan. My part is only to be willing to trust God – or the perfection which is now. It is only through willingness and trust that I can be aware of eternal peace and love. When I am aware of something, I do not question it. I see it truly. When I accept perfection as the only thing there is, I cease to interfere with it and to block its manifestation. I begin to be a channel or teacher of God. And what can bring forth a channel of God apart from inner peace and love all ways, always?

4. How can I heal myself?

In order to heal myself, I must understand what my healing has to be. This is because in the world of chaos I want to heal something which I believe is me and which in truth does not exist. The only way to be healed is through my awareness of my *sanity*. Here the word "health" is not used because health refers to a body. It is never a body that has to be healed. It is that part of our mind that we have made and with which we believe we think real thoughts.

The only way for that part of the mind to be healed is through the recognition that this part is not the real self and this is done through inner stillness. The word "inner" refers to that part of me which is neither the body nor the brain, that part which says "I". It is not seen, it is not explained, it is only felt and experienced. And it is there and only there that the healing has to occur.

The part of the mind that I have made, I have made it through striving. I have desired things that were not me and I have made every effort to get them. I must realize that this leads me to pain and then be willing for my mind to be healed. True healing is not a process leading a form from a wrong state to a right one. True healing is only of the mind. When a true healing manifests itself in a physical form it is only an effect of a healing that has taken place in the mind.

Why do I have to still my mind to be healed? To still my mind is to cease to believe that it can bring me something I need. In that state of stillness, I might have thoughts coming up, but I do not pay attention to them. I am willing to experience something new, something I do not know.

For this, I simply watch my projections. These projections are all the thoughts that come to me, related to the past or the future. They are all judgments. They tell me to strive, to look for something I should possess. They tell me that I might fail and that I have to strive more and more in order not to fail.

What has brought me pain is my judgmental state. When I judge, I set up levels or differences, thus accepting myself apart and different from what I judge. I judge because I perceive something wrong. What do I perceive in this world of illusion? I perceive what my physical eyes see: forms. I do not perceive God or Spirit. I perceive my brothers as bodies. I perceive myself and others as bodies. This is the only factor that reminds me somewhere, somehow, that we are alike. This is why my way out of the dream is done by watching what happens in my relationships according to my state of mind. I must see who my brother is to know who I am *because* I believe that we are both separate bodies. Now why is it not possible to perceive who I am without my brother?

This is because of the nature of my being and his. Our being is perfect love. This being is totally giving and sharing. I cannot grasp this intellectually. I cannot build up a theory about it. I have to *experience* this love. And how could love be experienced *alone*?

This is how my brother is truly my savior. I have to recognize that what I say and do to others, I say and do to myself. This is because what I say or do to my brother *is an effect* of my thinking. If what I say or do comes from a thought that is not real, a thought of separation, I separate myself more. I go deeper into a sense of separation, which always brings with it suffering and pain. But when what I say or do comes from a true loving thought, it allows me to experience a sense of love, a sense of joining. The happiness or sense of love that I experience comes back to me from the love I have offered. Through my interacting with my brother, I begin to understand that whatever I send out always comes back to me. This is the law of love. This is true sharing. It is the only sharing there is, and it gives me, while in this dream, a glimpse of the infinite joy of creation.

5. Who are the true miracle workers?

No one ever performs a miracle. A miracle happens in time at the perfect time when we are willing to let it happen. All miracles have already happened in truth as soon as the separation occurred. A miracle, which seems to happen in time, is merely the effect of a projection that is being undone. How is this projection undone? It is undone by the perfect judgment of Spirit that can only manifest itself through us when we are willing.

So it is our willingness and trust which make us appear as true miracle workers. As soon as we are willing to be a true miracle worker, we are one. When we say this, we speak in time. But we know that we all will eventually reach home *because* it is the Will of God that we be home. In that sense every one of us is already a true miracle worker, even if he does not appear to be one now.

Why do we say a "true" miracle worker? True means real and reality is pure love. Reality is being and not striving. In this world, the mind we have made by siding with the ego has a power of its own. By special training, it can achieve illusions of miracles. It can produce spectacles to induce belief for a purpose of its own. These "miracles" do not happen naturally, they are not true miracles because of their source which is the finite mind. They lead to more separation. Yet, as every illusion, they are used by Spirit in its own way.

A true miracle worker is anyone who is awakened. Anyone who is awakened is aware of his oneness with God. It appears in time that we are awakened only from time to time, in these instants when we are willing. This is true in the illusion of time. It is not true in reality. Given the fact that we are constantly one with God, whatever our state of awareness might be in time, as soon as we are willing, any miracle can be performed through us. There is no order of difficulty in miracles and there is no "big" or "small" miracle worker.

It appears for a time that some of us perform more miracles than others. These miracles might seem "bigger" or "harder" than others. This appears to be so only because we are afraid of miracles, and we are given in time the recognition of the miracles that are best for us. A miracle does not happen to induce belief. In Heaven there is no belief. You do not need to believe in God, yet you do need to *experience* God and you need to experience miracles.

On our way home, we are constantly both teachers and students. In the learning process, the teaching goes from a teacher to a student. A true teacher and a true student are the same because they have the same goal. Yet in time one seems more advanced than the other. This is only an illusion used in the teaching-learning process. A true teacher knows that he is not more advanced than his student. His student might seem to be drawn to him because he appears more advanced. However, the reason why someone is drawn to a teacher is only known by Spirit working out the whole plan. What matters for us is to understand that everyone is our teacher, even if for a time we feel drawn to concentrate on a particular teacher.

We do not have to strive to find a teacher. Just by being willing and by trusting do we allow Spirit to lead us where we are supposed to be. As more of us are now willing, we all experience what appears as a quickening in the plan. More of us today are aware of a great number of shifts which are taking place in time, and more miracles are experienced by more and more of us.

Miracles are natural. They often appear to be performed by a teacher but it has nothing to do with the teacher himself. Until present time, as few of us were advanced on the way home, we made idols out of miracle workers. We thought they had a power that we did not have. Now the time has come to recognize that a miracle is only the effect of a *joining*. And this joining takes place between two brothers who are equal in truth.

When you appear to perform a miracle, be sure that you did do nothing. Do recognize the Source of the miracle you see. If you think *you* heal a brother, let this illusion be corrected by the One

Who knows that no one has to be healed. And do know that if you think someone has to be healed, this someone is you, or rather your perception of healing has to be healed.

6. What are the qualities of a miracle worker?

A miracle worker is perfect like all his brothers, and being perfect, he has no quality but perfection. Yet in this world where differences are still perceived, a miracle worker shows forth the following qualities, which make him appear openly as a miracle worker right now.

Trust

Miracles have already happened in truth and the reason why they seem to be delayed is our lack of trust. So it is that the first quality of a miracle worker is trust. Trust is a word that is alien to the ego. The ego knows only of bargains: I trust someone *because* he has been "fair" to me. Trust is impossible for the world because finite forms have to deceive sooner or later because they are finite and not real. The ego cannot conceive of trusting all ways, always. Yet trust is the first quality of a miracle worker from which all others follow.

A miracle worker trusts his brother completely. He sees only perfection in him. He trusts the infinite power of love that God has given him when he was created. He goes beyond his body to join with him in a holy relationship, which is the only *real* relationship with him.

A miracle worker never tries to see a miracle or to work out a miracle. He trusts the perfection of the plan and he merely watches its unfolding.

Willingness

A miracle worker must be willing to be a miracle worker. He is willing to be truly helpful. His willingness comes from his trust. When he is fully trusting, he is fully willing to be right where he is. He does not look anymore for his own way. He has chosen to be led on the way and is willing to follow the way wherever it leads him.

He is willing for miracles to occur, whatever they might be, for he truly knows that there is no order of difficulty in miracles. Then the call on him is never too great. He is not concerned with the moment in time a miracle seems to happen. He is willing to offer any miracle at any moment because he is aware of the Source of any miracle. He is willing for anything that Spirit leads him to say or to do. He is truly a channel for God, for all His ways, always.

Inner Peace

A miracle worker is wholly peaceful. He knows he need do nothing. He knows he cannot fail, for it is not he who does the work but He Who sent him. This brings him inner peace. Peace becomes his constant experience. And this peace is shared through the love that he shares with his brothers. He knows that it is not necessary for him to be aware of the miracles which are performed through him. He might not appear outwardly to be a miracle worker, but his true inner peace is a sure sign that he is one. He does not attack. He is truly meek. His peace brings him unlimited strength.

A true sense of knowledge

A miracle worker is aware of his Self. He has a true sense of knowledge. He does not believe in a man-made god, a frightening idol that can reward or punish. He does not believe in sin. He knows what love is through experiencing it. He knows he is one with his brother and God. He knows that miracles are performed *through* him. He knows he is in the world but not of the world. He knows he is beyond his body.

Non-Judgmental

A miracle worker does not judge. He merely listens and listens and listens again. He constantly listens to God and his brother. He is like a child. He comes with no concepts, no preconceived ideas. He is constantly reborn. Everyday is his birth. Every event is an opportunity for him to give and receive total love. Because he does not judge, he finds no attraction to guilt. He walks the earth quietly, happily and peacefully. He fears nothing. He walks with the power of God because he sees with God's vision.

Open

A miracle worker never denies anything. He merely recognizes the truth everywhere. He is totally open. He is open to any call from any brother. He has no place in himself that he keeps hidden. He has no secret, nothing to hide. He is open to everything because he knows he is one with everything. He knows that when he shuts himself out of something, he is limiting himself. This is why, always welcoming his brother, he is a true host to God.

7. How can I recognize Spirit and God in the world?

I am used to recognize things in the world through my senses. Believing my body is myself, I see that my connection to the outer world is through seeing, tasting, touching, hearing and smelling. How can I recognize Spirit and God with this body? It is not possible. It must be, then, if I ever want to recognize Spirit and God in the world, I have to go beyond my body. How can I do this?

To go beyond my body means to go to a state where my experience does not depend on the body. What is the body? The body is a projection I have made and I have identified with it. I have incarnated in a body *because* I believed a body was necessary. Within this body, I keep projecting everything outside by seeing everything apart from me. To escape this process, I have to watch it. I have to understand what my projections are.

My projections are everything I believe real and outside of me. I project outside of myself all that I believe real through my "mind". This is how I make my world. My world is an illusion because that which I believe to be outside of me and real cannot be real. This is because I *am* real. Real means eternal, beyond time, indestructible and one with the universe. This is the gift of God given to me when I was created. With the separation, I began to identify with a body, which is separated

148

from what is not the body. With this body, I see a world separated from me. As I *am* real, even if I am not aware of being real, the world I see as separated from me cannot be real, because reality cannot be separated from itself. For the same reason, the body I see as separated from the world cannot be real.

This might seem frightful, but I must understand it to be willing to sense the universal flow. I must cease to believe that I can understand who I am with my finite mind.

God is at work in the world through Spirit, and being of God, I have the ability to see and sense the light. Yet, I can be aware of the light *only* when I cease to believe that any private thought I ever had or will ever have is true.

God, being all there is, is inside me and I am inside God. We are one. How can I pretend to recognize Spirit and God by projecting a god which is lacking me? When I do this, I project a god and a body that are not real.

I must be willing to grasp this *because* it is the truth. God is never perceived but only fully experienced as total love and oneness. Thinking one instant that I can be outside of God is this thought of separation which produces the whole world I see. The real world is pure light and at hand. I have never left it; but to be aware of it, I have to look for it where it is: inside me.

Inside me is not inside my body, it is where I can see and sense the light. And where can I see and sense the light if I do not see and sense it in my brother? I have to understand that my brother can only be the light of the world. Then and only then can I be truly willing to let Spirit show me that my brother is one with me. I have to trust beyond all I know for love or reality to reveal itself. I have to recognize that what is revealed to me is beyond words. It is pure being. It is the one universal experience beyond words. This is why everything and everyone is constantly teaching me what reality is by saying to me:

"I embody the total and complete perfection of God within me in this instant.
I AM GOD. I embody the Christ".

And to learn this lesson and know it is the truth, I am willing to, practice every day:

"Everyone I see is perfect".

Whenever I meet or talk to someone, I will say silently:

"I see only perfection in you."

CHAPTER SEVEN

GOING HOME AGAIN TO THAT PLACE WE NEVER LEFT

We are going home again, down that one path that we all know so well. We are going home, following the one divine tone of Spirit that we all know and recognize as ourselves. Now is the time to put down our games, to awaken from the dream.

GOING HOME AGAIN TO THAT PLACE WE NEVER LEFT

Like little children playing in a meadow, Jesus comes in the Christ light and gently takes our hands. He leads us to the God, Spirit we never left. We do not have to hear his calling, nor do we have to believe in his way. Jesus awaits us with infinite love and patience. When we doubt, he loves us. When we are afraid, he loves us. When we despair and cry, he loves us. When we want to commit suicide, he loves us. When we curse him and others, he loves us. He awaits our return with boundless love. He awaits because he is the shortest way home to our Father.

Like a loving brother, he puts out his hand in kindness beyond belief. We cannot imagine the love which is constantly pouring without end from the One Infinite Source. We call that Source God – but you may use any name – for all words are meaningless. The experience of the light, the love, which streams out constantly and steadily with unimaginable grace and brilliance is ours. It always all ways flows towards us unceasingly. God never punishes. He never removes or lessens His love for us. He loves us all, unconditionally. He radiates this love every second of our finite existence and beyond. It is an impossibility for God to stop loving us, for that is His essence. It is all that He is and all that He knows. He has no other reality. He knows not any other thing in the universe.

We are going home again, down that one path that we all know so well. We are going home, following the one divine tone of Spirit that we all know and recognize as ourselves. Now is the time to put down our games, to awaken from the dream. It is time to rejoice in the sunshine – to take the hand of your brother, gently and quietly – to begin the journey back home. Now we join in love and we begin one by one to approach infinity. We begin to feel the light, the warmth of God's love and we open, at first with fear, and later with extreme gratefulness. We go step by step, closer and closer to the Source of love. Each step, we put down our desires, our masks, our games, our illusions, and we move without ceasing, closer and closer each moment, each day.

There is no choice and we know it. We know it. We must now go home to the place that we never left.

Nothing else is real. Nothing else matters.

I put out my hand to you – gently take it in complete trust. I am a child too. I do not know more than you. I do not know the way home. I trust. I trust in God that I know to be all loving, all love.

Take my hand now and let us go home together.
Let us rejoice in the happiness and joy
that is present in the moment.
Let us go home in love.
Let us go home.
Let us go.
Let us.
Let
Love

ADDENDUM

I trust in God's plan for me, knowing that He alone knows what is best for me.

ADDENDUM

1. Fragments of messages from Jesus taken down in 2010

1.1 It's just an illusion

You are changing. You are evolving. You are consciously moving into the light. Give me your burdens; give me your pain. I will toss them up in the air like balls used by a juggler to entertain the crowds. Those things that apparently make you hurt and suffer are simply your own little idle imaginings.

Come join me. Join the circus. Let us ride on the backs of elephants. Let us jump through rings of fire together. That way we can surmount the illusion and amuse ourselves at the same time.

Nothing is too difficult for the son or daughter of God when s/he holds my hand.

1.2   See in your brother and sister what you would have them be.

If you see kindness, they will be kind. If you see openness and flexibility, they will show you these qualities. If you see love, they will become love beings. Look beyond appearances to see what your brother and sister are in truth: pure love beings.

When I look at you, I do not see your faults, your frustrations, your limits, nor your fears. I look upon you as the pure love and light that you are. How could it be otherwise since I see with God's eyes? By seeing you as you really are and by giving no validity to your ego's fears, you are healed. See yourself through God's eyes. Go beyond your ego vision and you will be healed as you heal others by seeing them in the same way.

1.3 *You are the light of the world*

You are the light of the world. Let your light shine, not only within yourselves, but let it radiate out to everyone and all things.

There are so many brothers and sisters that are crying out in the deserts of their souls. Will you not be open to be my servants so that everyone can finally recognize his true essence?

This is the work, the only work. I need you to be the hands of Spirit so that my mission may be completed. The love that you share is not special, it is who and what you are. This love will be so valued by all of those who are still suffering - who do not realize that they too can live constantly in my energy, in love.

What you cannot do alone, you will be able to accomplish together.

This last thought is the one that will help you the most in these coming days.

1.4 *He is here now!*

"I am the light and love of the world. 2000 years ago people were less conscious and they make the mistake of following me and not the message."

His return is not physical, but will occur in our hearts – and he is here now!

He is always with us and never leaves us alone.

1.5   *Now is the time.*

(I am awakened by an overwhelming feeling of love. Jesus is here.)

Dearest beloved child, do you know how precious you are to me? Your every word, your every thought, your every action is a blessing to me. Each time you express love for your brother or sister, you are blessing the entire world.

Walk in gratitude; bathe in love. When you swim in the river of truth, it can but lead you to one place, to that holy place within that you have never left.

I say to you now is the time and this is the place. When two or more are gathered in my name, miracles happen.

Do not be afraid to put your weapons of attack down, to allow yourself to enter upon sacred ground. I am with you on this apparent journey which leads nowhere. You are safe. You are protected. Come now, like a little child resting in the arms of his loving mother. Come now and put your burdens at my feet, for there is no greater love. It is through love that your lives are transformed. When you leave your problems with me, you are free to be the love that you are.

Oh, my child, if you could only know with what

love your purity is expressed. Take my hand and leave the rest behind. You are free. You are as God created thee. You are love. You are the light of the world.

1.6   *I wish to see with the eyes of God*

Listen to the voice of God. See with the eyes of God and speak with His voice, for what would God have you see and say when you gaze upon your brother who is all good? Would you say harsh words or would you place a loving hand upon his shoulder while he cries away his past?

When you are ready to see and live in heaven on earth, then you will see everything and everyone in the light of love.

There is only one will and that is of the Father as all other willing is the expression of ego. Do not let your ego and its sly ways allow you to miss one second of loving your brother who stands before you with great patience.

When you recognize who you truly are, you will instantly know that there is no one and nothing standing before you except the world that you falsely believed to be real. So go now and pick up the pieces of your scattered dreams. Place them upon the holy altar of God and allow Him to repair your poor little creation. For it is with the Holy Spirit that you will be given the courage to live the dream of reality, which is so much more than you could ever envision with your human eyes.

The time is now, for there is only the present moment and it is in the moment of now that you are able to seek the kingdom of God.

I wish to see that which is true with the eyes of God.

There is a lake covered in fog and you are standing at its edge. Somehow you do not believe the lake exists because you are unable to see the water. Gradually the fog lifts and then not only do you see the lake filled with calm blue water, but you are aware of a small island in its middle. There is erected a golden statue, representing the inner peace and true happiness which is all that you seek. You are standing on the shore of reality and you do not dare to get in a boat, which awaits you on the shore, to sail home. So go now. Bravery and courage are not needed. You need but believe. You need but be willing and the peace that you seek shall flow into your hearts, as easily as a bird flies across a sunlit sky.

I wish to see with the eyes of God.

1.7. *You are my hands on earth.*

You are my hands on earth. Even though you may not understand fully that you are within the illusion, you can understand that these words are real and meaningful (within it). Please gather together in my name and serve as a pure channel for my energy.

This energy is pure light and pure love. It is a gift to humanity. You do not need to be courageous. You do not need to trust. In whom would you trust – certainly not that small powerless ego that you identify as *yourself.* Trust in who you really are – trust in me. Even though *A Course in Miracles* is an illusion, it's a pretty useful tool, wouldn't you agree? All ways are used, yet all ways are meaningless. You are important. You are needed, and then again, you are not needed and you are not important. Do you understand?

Everything and everyone is being used to aid you in the remembrance of who you truly are. And who are you in reality? Look around the room. Look at the others that you think exist. Who is there? If you still see men and women, some more attractive than others, you are not seeing with my eyes. Everyone before you will disappear the moment you realize that you are pure love and pure light. Whom could you not love when you see the world you created with my eyes?

Look upon everyone as yourself, for there is no one outside of you. Every person that you see before you is but a mirror of your state. If you are sad, you will see sadness. If you are judgmental, you will be judged. If you are filled with love and joy, you will create only happy people around you.

This is the gift of living in the illusion. Change your thoughts, your expectations, or your glasses and you will perceive differently. Why not become who you really are? Why not see everyone and everything with my eyes?

Know that you are my precious creation. You are nothing and you are everything. You are pure love. This is the essence of your being. Rest in the arms of love and open your heart to fully accept the love beings whom I have sent you. They are present to remind you of the love that you are. Do not close the door to what you are. The love, which is coming toward you, is being sent to you by me, and yet you still create in the illusion.

Dear sister/brother, take my hand and come home to that place which you never left. You are pure love. You are the light of the world.

1.8   The kingdom is within

Each time two or more are gathered in my name, with purity of heart, there is greater joy in the universe. Each time two or more remember that they are not separated, that the physical is only an illusion, there is great joy. Each time there is a gathering in my name, there is great joy.

Who would not want to willingly put his ego down if he only but knew that beyond it lies riches which are greater than anything to be found in the illusion. The real treasures of existence are not to be found in that lonely world which you have created out of fear, rejection, and separation. There is nothing which shines as brightly as the light of God, even though the futile attempt to search for gold continues on the earth which you created. Do you still believe that you are more powerful than God?   Have you found any satisfaction which is lasting in that which you falsely seek in His name?

My dear brothers and sister, search no further because that which you seek cannot be found outside of yourselves. The kingdom is within. It is in silence that you will find it.   The holy relationship is within you. Please have confidence, not in yourselves, for that can never be, for the small self does not exist even though the ego will do everything to convince you that it does.

The Holy Spirit is present to guide you. You know the way. It is fulfilling. It is peaceful. It is filled with fragrant roses and the nourishment that you have forever sought. Please join me in the holy triangle, so that you too may radiate that which you are.

1.9   *Trust*

Who could you not trust when in truth there is no one outside of yourself?

Do you not trust me, your beloved brother, to guide you home in the meantime?

Are you not willing to see every brother as your savior?

Do you still believe that the past will repeat itself?

The key word for the next few days is "trust". When you find your head filled with thoughts, which will lead you nowhere except further into the illusion, attempt to stop and go to trust. Whenever this occurs, know that you are not in truth, and simply repeat the following phrase until heavenly peace is once again restored to you.

"I trust in God's plan for me, knowing that He alone knows what is best for me."

2. Phoebe's Final vision in 2011

Jesus, who has waited so patiently on the stairs into the kingdom, smiles down at me as he extends his hand. I feel that I've kept him waiting more than twenty years to give birth to this book. He says:

Oh, no, my dearest one, you have not kept anyone waiting. I could not be born again into the world of your illusion before human consciousness was ready. The appearance of this book will make a difference as does every creation inspired by God.

Was it not worth my coming to earth 2000 years ago? I did not come to atone for your sins, as the church will tell you. I came to take you home, right now in this moment. I am always willing to take the hand of any brother or sister who shares my vision. Let's dance in the meadows and share our love.

I did not come to earth to suffer, to be crucified. I came to be resurrected, to teach about love. Until you love every single one of your brothers and sisters, you will continue to suffer. So love one another. That's my message. Take each other in your arms and embrace. Wipe away all tears. Kiss each other. See that you are all innocent little children crying out for love.

Soar to the heavens. Twinkle in the skies. Sing

like the birds swaying high on the tree branches. Kiss the earth. Then laugh, I mean really laugh at the wonders of the illusion you have created.

When you are through with all that nonsense, come home and live the truth. Just wait, you too will be struck by the lightning of the truth, just when you least expect it.

And then Jesus danced and pulled me into the miracle of reality with a great big belly laugh!

That's it. That's all there is to say and it's enough!

You are the light of the world.
Let your light shine,
not only within yourselves,
but let it radiate out
to everyone and all things.

CLARIFICATION OF TERMS

Clarifying a term is not defining a term. The concept of defining a term is an illusion. A term is a concept that refers to the past, to something we have taught ourselves. To define a term is to use other illusory concepts in order to give it a "precise" definition. We do this by using our finite mind which cannot know what is real. This is why a universal theology is impossible.

However, we know what consistency is within a belief system. It is something that does not contradict within its own range. In our world we call this reason. And reason will help us to clarify the terms we use. If we are willing to bring to the light *all* parts of our belief system, reason will show us that its cornerstone is a lie, or rather an illusion.

Then, we will be willing to go beyond our belief system, to go beyond words and their meaning. We will be willing to let the unknown be revealed to us through our everyday life. We will be willing to experience the simplicity and the infinite magnitude of our being.

In order to be more consistent with the terms we use, let us now clarify seven major ones used in this book.

1. GOD

The word God refers to the Cause of creation. This Cause is beyond creation. It is a Thought that exists in timelessness because It is pure infinite Love. It does not exist apart from other real thoughts. Yet all other real thoughts exist and are real because they are created by the One First Thought and never leave their Source.

God is infinite Love and nothing else but Love. The concept of Love implies infinite giving and infinite receiving. All that exists has to be Love. To understand that this has to be true, let us imagine something which is real. This something cannot be a form, because a form is always limited whatever its dimension may be. Beyond the limits of this form there would be a void *lacking* this form. Then we could not speak of infinity. So it is that this something which is real and infinite has to be Spirit. And what is Spirit if not a thought?

Now we have a thought which is infinite, beyond time, and which cannot be threatened because it is infinite. Let us imagine what would happen if this thought were not totally loving. At this place where it would not be loving, it would fear. And what could it fear except something which is not itself? If this something that is not itself were real, we would have something real apart from infinity. This contradicts.

God is a word used for infinity, perfection or reality. It is often used instead of these terms because, within a finite mind, it generally holds the concept of infinite love. Because God is infinite, God is not perceived but experienced. If infinity is real, who can be real and apart from infinity? No one. And if you are real, you must be God Himself expressing Himself *as* you. This you cannot understand. You can only be aware of it and you will be fully aware of it when you are back home to knowledge – or Heaven, to that place of infinite bliss and ecstasy which you never left.

2. CREATION

Creation is the effect of God. It is the law of God. Creation is the infinite sharing of the One First Thought. Creation is infinite extension because a real thought extends indefinitely without leaving its Source. For our finite mind, creation seems to imply a multiple projection. It seems to be somewhere, somehow the loss of Oneness. It appears to be a projection *outside*. Our belief in the possibility of separation – of infinite sharing not being infinite – has veiled our awareness of being ever creating.

Creation is infinite oneness and infinite multiplicity at the same "time". Creation is beyond time in timelessness. Creation is the One First Thought extending Itself for ever *now*. Creation is the infinite movement of Love in perfect stillness.

3. MIRACLES

Miracles are in the world but not of the world. They are necessary in time for the undoing of our illusions which made the world as we see it. They come from our Source, they come from our Mind, the one Mind.

Miracles do not matter as such because they are temporary. However, they are required for our way home. Or rather, we have to become gradually aware of them along our way home.

Miracles are an illusion. Yet, they are the only illusion that leads to reality, because they are the only illusion that comes from love. They happen automatically when we are somewhere, somehow, open to love. They happen through forgiveness.

Because they come from love, they are shared by the entire universe. Because they transcend time, their effect is seen in time but they all have already happened in truth. We can say that they all happened when the thought of separation occurred. However, we can also say that, as the past does not really exist, the thought of separation never really occurred and so the miracles. This is why they are a teaching device which is used in time as long as time is necessary for learning. In Heaven, there is no miracle.

4. AWAKENING

To awaken is to shift from illusion to the awareness of reality. An illusion exists *for* the finite mind. Reality exists *as* the one Mind.

When we are in a desert, our physical eyes might see a lake in the distance. Yet, if we know the desert, we will truly say, "It is an illusion", meaning "It appears to be a lake, but I know it is only sand". Then, this illusion is no longer an illusion for us. It has gone back to nothingness.

We are now asleep and dreaming because we believe in one illusion which is real *for* us. This illusion is the belief that we are separated from all that which is not us. To awaken from this illusion, we must know who we are and experience our Self. We must go inside ourselves, listen to our Self, trust our Mind and gradually awaken to the awareness of love's presence.

This awakening appears to come step by step. These steps are the removal of that which blocks. It seems that our illusions disappear one by one. Yet, it is constantly the same process at work in time. This continuing process produces a gradual shift from a nightmare to a happy dream. The end of the process is a sudden shift from perception to knowledge or Christ consciousness.

5. ATONEMENT

Atonement is the vision of Christ. It is the vision of God and His beloved Son as one. It is the last miracle to be seen. Atonement is the end of our journey home. It is the last step already taken by God, but which appears *to us* to be taken in time.

As long as we are in the dream of separation, there seems to be one atonement for each one of us. Yet, when we become suddenly aware that "our" atonement has taken place, Atonement is seen as a concept in time referring to the recognition of God experiencing Himself. It is the thinking of the universe recognizing itself through an ever increasing joy. Atonement has disappeared and it has dissolved in the eternal experience of bliss and ecstasy. Everyone and everything is seen home and perfectly safe as time is transcended.

6. CHRIST

Christ is another term for the perfect Son of God, one with His Father. You are the Christ. Christ consciousness is the highest state of consciousness and Jesus attained this state. We made an idol of him, because we did not see that we and Jesus were all equal brothers. This mistake is wholly understandable when we see that the concept of infinite love is totally alien to our finite mind.

Jesus kept saying key words such as: "I of my own self can do nothing", "I and the Father are one", or "The Kingdom of Heaven is within you".

During his lifetime, Jesus was demonstrating the way home for each one of us as an elder brother. He had fully grasped the principle of oneness and the law of infinity. He was a perfect example of an extreme situation where perfect forgiveness was demonstrated out of perfect unconditional love.

Now the time has come for Christ to reappear on earth *because* many of us are being prepared by Spirit to acknowledge His Presence, which has always been there. Now is the time for many of us to go home together, to attain Christ consciousness, or the full awareness of being the one Son of God. This can only be done by seeing the face of Christ in all our brothers.

7. HEAVEN

Heaven is our home that we never left. We have given ourselves the illusion that we left our home when we began to reflect upon ourselves and to see ourselves as separate entities. This has led us to the belief in good and evil.

This "unthinkable" thought made our separation real *to us*. Then we began to dream and to build up, through the power of our thoughts, the world as we see it. However, this is only a dream, an illusion, and it has ever kept us from being in Heaven.

In Heaven we are beyond time. We create without limits, extending ourselves as Spirit, one with God, *as* God. Our journey back home is an illusion, but it is *necessary* for us to undertake it and, when it ends, to become aware that it was an illusion. The journey away from Heaven began when we forgot to laugh. The journey back will end in a happy laughter.

AUTHORS

To know more about the authors or their activities, please email them:

Sylvain du Boullay: sylvainduboullay@gmail.com

Phoebe Lauren: phoebe.lauren@yahoo.com

Made in the USA
Charleston, SC
25 July 2011